Not All
Soldiers
Wore Pants

Not All Soldiers Wore Pants

A Witty World War II WAC Tells All

by Rose Rosenthal

Ryzell Books
Rochelle Park, New Jersey

Library of Congress Cataloging-in-Publication Data

Rosenthal, Rose.
    Not all soldiers wore pants: witty World War II WAC
tells all / by Rose Rosenthal
    p. cm
    ISBN 0-9636931-0-7
    1. Rosenthal, Rose.   2. United States. Army. Women's
Army Corps—History.   3. World War, 1939–1945—
Personal narratives, American.   4. United States. Army—
Biography.   5. Women's soldiers—United States—
Biography.   I. Title
D769.39.R67   1993   940.54'8173
                                        QBI93-836

Published in the United States by Ryzell Books
PO Box 246
Rochelle Park, NJ 07662-0246

Manufactured in the United States of America
Book design and production by Kramer Communications
Printed on recycled paper by Thomson-Shore

First Edition

Second Printing - 1995

My maiden name appears throughout the text. The names of other persons have been changed, as have certain identifying characteristics.

Not All Soldiers Wore Pants

My thanks to George, who liked my story and encouraged me to share it.

My thanks to Mil for pointing me in the right direction and guiding me in — I can't count the ways.

And my special thanks to the many WACs with whom I served whose friendship gave me so much.

Foreword

Not so long ago, a woman from Michigan wrote me the following:

"I'm 71 now and remember World War II very well. I knew a lot of women who were nurses and those who did other things.

"I've been reading a lot about World War II now that old papers have been declassified and our men who were in the war are writing about it.

"Are there books written by nurses or other women who were in the War? I've read over 100 books this past year published since the early 1980s and only one even mentioned nurses. It mentioned that the nurses came after the battle and the island was under control. That was the Pacific. Nothing was mentioned in any of the others I read."

Thankfully, the coffers are starting to swell. Not only are women who served in World War II as nurses writing of their experiences in a new and different world, but so are the women who served in many other capacities as well. I'm continually surprised at the number of people I meet who still don't realize women were in the military during World War II and that they played not just a significant, but historic, role.

Not All Soldiers Wore Pants fills a special void for veterans like me and for those who serve today. It helps put our experiences in perspective with those who paved the way for us. And for all people interested in the contributions of women to our nation's defense, this book helps relieve a severe shortage of research material about the subject.

It wasn't easy for the first women who reported for training as new recruits. First, they had to survive discussions with family and friends, who usually tried to discourage them from enlisting. Once they did, uniforms were not available, and housing facilities were still being adapted for women. The women were different from male recruits in that most, like Rose, were older, professional women who had at least one college degree. To say that it was difficult to room with 40 or so other women in a room furnished only with Army bunk beds and small clothing lockers would be putting it mildly. And training was a shock to their systems. Every aspect of life had to have been a challenge. Rose Rosenthal describes all these aspects with the sense of humor she and others needed to make it through.

Since Rose was selected for officer's training, we can follow her through experiences not only as an enlisted woman but as a junior officer as well. From her interactions with other members of the Women's Army Corps, to her encounters with men and women along the way, we get an intimate look at what life was like for these pioneering women.

— Wilma L. Vaught
Brigadier General, USAF (Ret.)

Prologue

On May 14, 1992, I hung the American flag out my fifth-floor window overlooking Hackensack's Prospect Avenue and its curious passers-by.

My twenty-eight-year-old neighbor asked, "What's the flag for?"

"Today's a holiday," I answered. "Today marks fifty years since the birth of our WAACs."

"Our wax? Like floor wax? I didn't know we had a holiday for that too."

What a pity! One hundred thousand devoted women gave up jobs, family, friends, and the comforts of home to assist in achieving our World War II victory. Yes, they served in Europe, the Middle East, China, Burma, India, North Africa, Egypt, and New Caledonia. Yet people in the next generations scratch their heads and rush to the encyclopedia when working a crossword puzzle and encountering "World War II army women — four letters."

I had considered some other forms of celebration. A parade with wildly cheering spectators would have been nice. But could I round up enough former WAACs and WACs to converge for a parade? I suppose I could have paraded down Main Street by myself in my Eisenhower jacket, which now misses closing by eight inches, proudly carrying the American flag over my shoulder. Wisely, I recognized that instead of hearing wildly cheering spectators, I'd be more apt to hear, "Who's the nut?"

I even considered renting a billboard in Times Square showing a WAC (preferably me) striking a pose over giant letters reading, "SHE DID HER SHARE," or hiring a skywriter whose puffs would spell out, "HEAR, HEAR, WE SALUTE THE WAACS OF YESTERYEAR." But I had to concede the likelihood of achieving success in those areas was minimal.

Still, I knew displaying the flag just wasn't enough, especially since I could see perplexed passers-by looking up at my flag and deciding there was something wrong with my calendar.

So I decided to write a book. We hear much about the women who served in Korea, Vietnam, and the Persian Gulf—and rightly so. But we should also hear about the eighty-five thousand army women of World War II who served so nobly on army posts all over the United States and the seventeen thousand who served overseas.

Of course, I don't see myself in a class with Norman Mailer, Irwin Shaw, and John Hersey. They wrote exciting accounts of incredible bravery under fire: of soldiers who, with the enemy breathing down their necks, crawled under barbed wire to safety; of fearless heroes who captured enemy-infested hills singlehanded. Heck, I didn't do any of those things. However, I did help. I released a man for combat duty, and — who knows? — maybe he was the one who carried the flag to the top of Mount Surabachi.

Some days, when I have poured a quarter-cup of bay leaves into my potato soup because I thought the jar said celery leaves and when the phone has rung four times and there's no one there and the one time I do get a call it's the bank telling me I've overdrawn my account, I feel a need for some morale-building fantasy. That's when I like to think my man was Dwight David Eisenhower, and that, but for me, countless battles might never have been won and the Eisenhower jacket might never have been known to the human race.

But what would I call my book? Night after night, I'd put on my pajamas and sit in the den, trying to craft a succinct phrase that might catch the eye of a book browser. No luck. Then one night, sitting in the den drinking iced coffee, I began to feel uncomfortable. My air-conditioning wasn't working, and it was the hottest day of the summer (which, natch, is always when the air-conditioning isn't working). I simply had to do something for relief, so I removed my pajama bottoms. (Fortunately, the top was one of those long jobs, so I didn't stick to the Naugahyde chairs.) Now, this was no earth-shattering act. Under ordinary circumstances, I would never have remembered it. But something clicked. Suddenly words started to dance around in my head, and out waltzed: NOT ALL SOLDIERS WORE PANTS.

Now, I don't want anyone to misinterpret my title. It doesn't mean our soldiers were running around half-naked. Uh-uh, I intend no salacious implications. This book is about me and the WAAC/WACs.

CHAPTER ONE

Pigeons, Please
Don't Catch Cold

In Great Britain, women were operating aircraft guns and ferrying planes. In Russia, they were performing all the duties of warfare. The United States had no women's army when World War II started.

On December 7, 1941, the situation changed. After the Japanese attacked Pearl Harbor and President Roosevelt declared our country at war, Edith Nourse Rogers, congresswoman from Massachusetts, introduced a bill in the House of Representatives to establish the Women's Army Auxiliary Corps.

Now, for the first time, our lawmakers began to give serious consideration to the introduction of women into this jealously guarded realm of violence which, through the ages, tradition had kept within the male province.

It wasn't Congresswoman Rogers' intent to put guns into the hands of women, usurping men's great privilege of killing. No. Women were to be inducted into the service for the sole purpose of releasing behind-the-lines soldiers for combat duty.

Even today, the magnitude of this project boggles the mind. Creating a women's army meant teaching women to cook and bake by the ton; it meant training schoolteachers, secretaries, sales clerks, athletes, actresses, and factory workers to be office clerks, telephone operators, administrative specialists, airplane spotters, cartographers, and truck drivers.

Although the Women's Army Auxiliary Corps was the first organized women's army, it was not the first time women had actively participated in war. The Army Nurse Corps, in existence since 1901, had seven thousand members at the outbreak of the war, and the Navy Nurse Corps, established in 1908, had seven hundred members. True, they were already adequately trained for their work, and even the future enlistees would come into the Corps without the need for further training, for whether the thermometer is placed into the mouth, or wherever — in Kalamazoo, Michigan, or in the Tuamato Archipelago — thermometers, mouths, and wherevers are pretty much the same the world over.

Also, as civilians, the women of America have always made significant contributions in wartime. During World War I, women called Marinettes did clerical work for the Marines; our women have run canteens, driven ambulances, rolled bandages, knitted sweaters, and worked in munitions factories. Indeed, history books even describe the occasional presence of a woman on the battlefield.

For instance, Mary Ludwig Hays ran back and forth among the wounded soldiers at the battle of

Monmouth during the Revolution, dispensing water as she went, and thus is recorded in history as Molly Pitcher.

There was also Deborah Sampson. Using the name Robert Shurtleff, she served in the Continental Army for three years disguised as a man. Despite the fact that several times she acquired wounds that required the services of a doctor, her disguise went undetected. Only when she was seized with brain fever during the Yorktown campaign was her sex discovered.

Here I must pause to wonder. It's not that I question the accuracy of the history books. It's just that in the case of Deborah Sampson, a.k.a. Robert Shurtleff, I find certain questions popping into my mind. How did she manage to be so private in a milieu where availability of privacy would rank zero on a scale of one to ten? And how did she manage privacy for three years during those eliminatory performances in which body position would be a dead giveaway? And what was with those crazy doctors? Were they blind, or did she catch her brain fever from them? How did she manage to keep far away from the men under all kinds of situations that might have revealed her sex? Didn't they notice when she removed her clothing that there was something different about him/her? Could it be she never removed her clothing during those three years? If so, that would explain why the men knew so little about her body conformation. They avoided her like the plague, especially on days when the wind was blowing in their direction.

In May 1942, when President Roosevelt signed
Congresswoman Rogers' bill into law, thousands of
women responded to the call. Pearl Harbor had been
attacked; Americans were outraged; we were a country
at war, and the women let it be known in no uncertain
terms that they were part and parcel of it.

Applications poured into the recruiting centers
from every part of the country: from executives in
Detroit, Michigan, and Pittsburgh, Pennsylvania; from
dieticians in Londonderry, Vermont, and Columbus,
Ohio; from schoolteachers in Englewood, New Jersey,
and Houston, Texas. There were applications from
sweethearts and wives of men in service; from women
who saw the opportunity to combine patriotism with
escape from boring jobs; and applications from the
victims of domineering mothers, broken romances,
and loneliness.

The male population reacted.

"The most ridiculous bill I ever encountered.
Release a man for active duty? Hogwash!" declared a
congressman from North Carolina.

"The silliest piece of legislation I have ever seen,"
screamed a congressman from New York.

"How nice! Shall we dance?" sneered a regular
army First Sergeant.

"Damn it all! First they send dogs; now it's wom-
en," protested the commanding officer of a base for
special combat tactics.

The GIs, on the other hand, were ambivalent.
They weren't exactly infatuated with the idea of being
released to a foxhole, but they could see interesting

potential. They envisioned hearing at the Post Exchange: "Sorry, no shaving cream. We have cold cream, cleansing cream, hand cream, leg cream, body cream, rouge cream, ice cream, and sour cream — but *no* shaving cream." The GIs pondered this probable deprivation but imagined a tradeoff for a lark in the dark. As a matter of fact, they coined that well-known epigram, "A scratchy lark is better than no lark."

When the WAAC bill was signed, I was teaching eighth grade in a public elementary school. I enjoyed my work, but I didn't see showing thirteen-year-olds how to compute interest by the sixty-day, 6 percent method as my lifetime career. I had planned to teach for a year or two, then to get married and have babies, preferably in that order. Certainly it was not my plan to teach for umpteen years. As it happened, I had already been teaching more umps than I had anticipated.

The ruination of my timetable coupled with my outrage at the Pearl Harbor attack led me to give serious thought to joining the Women's Army Auxiliary Corps. I spent sleepless nights grappling with the implications.

One just doesn't, with a plunge, sacrifice a comfortable existence at home for the vicissitudes of army life. True, with all the men gone, there wasn't much life at home, and the army might conceivably provide some interesting vicissitudes; yet I had many misgivings.

How would I adjust to communal living — being domiciled in one room with a swarm of jabbering females? How would I react to being ordered early to bed and early to rise by a bugle whose plaintive notes piercing the darkness of the late evening could be extremely moving, but whose plaintive notes piercing the darkness of the early morning could be a pain in the ass? How would I feel not being able to check out if I didn't like the crowd? What would I do if I got homesick? I recall a conversation I had with my cousin, Lil.

"You know how much I hate chicken soup," I said.

"Yes. So?"

"Well, I'm afraid that come Friday nights, I'll simply die if I can't have some nice, home-made chicken soup. Now you have to admit, that's getting pretty darn homesick."

"Tell you what," answered Lil. "Every Friday night I'll send you some nice, home-made chicken soup that you can hate."

"Oh, really? And how will you manage that? By carrier pigeon?"

"Hey, that's a good idea. I'll find a nice Jewish carrier pigeon to carry your nice Jewish chicken soup."

"Well, make sure he's of the Reform movement. An Orthodox pigeon won't fly on Friday night."

"Stop worrying. I'll take care of everything. I'll even make sure to get one that doesn't have a cold, so he won't eat your chicken soup en route."

"Well, I guess you took care of that problem for me."

"Glad to help. Anything else?" asked Lil.

"Yes, since you ask. I hear they blow a whistle and

yell, 'EVERYBODY TO THE BATHROOM!' What are you going to do about that?"

"Armies don't have bathrooms."

"What?" I shrieked. "You're kidding."

"They have latrines."

"Oh. Thank God."

While I was wrestling with my innumerable doubts, recruiting for officer candidates started. Initially, the Women's Army Auxiliary Corps would recruit twenty-five thousand women, and ultimately one hundred thousand. But first, four hundred and forty women were to be selected to make up the first three officer candidate classes. Subsequently, five more classes would be drawn from civilian life and trained by male officers at Fort Des Moines, Iowa, the post selected by the War Department to be the first WAAC training center. With only twelve hundred women from the entire country to be picked as officer candidates, and with a specific number allotted to each of the nine Corps Areas, if I was giving any thought to applying for Officer Candidate School, I had to make up my mind quickly.

My problem was that I wasn't quite sure whether I preferred to be an enlisted woman or an officer. On one hand, I could be an efficient underling without too much responsibility, but I'd have to be resigned to permanent mass living. Or I could aspire to the burdens and responsibilities of command but have the sweet luxury of privacy. I had heard that Generals even had their own latrines, a feature I found tremendously attractive, having been reared in a family of five children, two parents, and one bathroom. Not that I had any delusions I could attain such heights. If the truth be told, it occurred to me that the Army General Classification Test might reveal I was better equipped for cleaning a latrine than having one.

I wasn't concerned about the other requirements. I exceeded the minimum in every category. I was five feet tall plus; I weighed 105 pounds plus; I was a high school graduate plus; I was twenty-one plus; I was in good health; my character was excellent (I told little white lies only occasionally).

But I was really in a dilemma. I was supposed to arrive at a decision quickly as to whether I wanted to be a WAAC officer before I had arrived at the decision as to whether I wanted to be a WAAC at all. I just didn't know what to do. Then one day I had help from an unexpected quarter. On June 1, three days before the cut-off date for the recruitment of officers, our local newspaper, in two-inch headlines, blazoned, "CREAM OF AMERICAN WOMANHOOD TO BECOME OFFICERS IN THE WAAC."

That did it. Not by the wildest stretch of the imagination could I metaphor myself into cream. Maybe a little half-and-half. But cream? Never!

Many months later, after I had met the "cream of American womanhood," I realized I had interpreted the newspaper headline too strictly. Not that there wasn't a lot of cream; there was. But there was also much half-and-half, and considerable skim milk. Perhaps I should have realized the choice of those particular words might have been made by an overworked editor with a deadline to meet who had wrestled with his headline all night. At the breakfast table, exhausted from lack of sleep and cursing the day he chose newspaper work for his profession, his bleary-eyed gaze rests on the carton of sweet cream he has for breakfast each morning with Rice Krispies and bananas.

"THAT'S IT!" he shouts. "CREAM OF AMERICAN WOMANHOOD!" He does a solo conga around the kitchen table, snapping his fingers overhead and chanting rhythmically, "One-two-three-GOOD. Cream of American Woman-HOOD. One-two-three GOOD. Cream of American woman-HOOD."

Well, it may have been GOOD for old Twinkle-Toes. But it sure scared hell out of me.

At least it helped me solve *that* problem. I put all thoughts of becoming an officer behind me.

Fortunately for the WAAC, not all women were intimidated by newspaper headlines. On the first day alone, recruiting officers throughout the country distributed 13,208 application blanks — pink for girls.

CHAPTER TWO

Some Hunk!

By the time school closed that summer of 1942, 450 officer candidates were already wearing down their GI heels on the grassy parade ground of Fort Des Moines, Iowa. Recruiting for enlisted women was scheduled to start after the final five officer candidate classes had been selected from civilian life, and this procedure had not yet been completed.

I decided I needed to get away for a short time to think in unfamiliar surroundings — away from family and friends who might discourage me if I were to confide in them. The surroundings I chose were in Philadelphia, Pennsylvania, the home of Betsy Ross, the Liberty Bell, the First Continental Congress, and the Cream Cheese in the Silver and Blue Paper. Perhaps visits to these historic places would help relegate to insignificance the jabbering females, the multiple stalls called latrines, and the morning bugle.

I arrived in that City of Brotherly Love on a Friday afternoon and rented a room at the Young Women's Christian Association (YWCA), which a friend had recommended as clean, convenient, and cheap. Had I spent months looking for a place to simulate army living, I couldn't have made a better choice. There were loads of jabbering females, multiple stalls (called johns instead of latrines), and a next-door neighbor who snored like a morning bugle.

On the very day I arrived, the newspapers announced recruiting for enlisted women would begin on the following Monday.

For three days I lay on my bed staring up at the ceiling, which stared right back at me without giving me an answer. On Monday morning I asked the young lady in the lobby to direct me to the recruiting building — not to enlist in it, just to pass it. I'm not quite sure what I expected to happen. Maybe that the sight of Uncle Sam pointing his finger and saying "The army needs you!" would give me the push I needed, or that a big hook would reach out and drag me in, relieving me of this exhausting problem of making a decision. But neither happened. There was no hook, and Uncle Sam did nothing for me, perhaps because someone had drawn a mustache on him.

Monday passed — the first recruiting day. Then that night I had a dream. I was one of a long line of women in front of a grilled window behind which sat Uncle Sam. As each woman approached the window, Uncle Sam handed her a pink paper. She saluted, asked "May I?" took two giant steps forward and disappeared into a foxhole. When my turn came, I stepped forward, reached out my hand, and Uncle Sam said, "Sorry. None left. Come back next war," and shut the window in my face.

I awoke with a start. I leaped out of bed and got dressed lickety-split. I wouldn't risk the two-hour trip home but instead raced the eight blocks to the recruiting station like Roger Bannister breaking the world's record for the mile run — which was really quite silly, considering it was six o'clock in the morning. Needless to say, when the doors opened three hours later, I was first on line.

Fearfully, I said to the Corporal in charge, "Do you have any left?"

"Any what left?"

"Application blanks."

"A few," he answered as he reached over and pulled a pink paper from a stack a mile high.

I sat down at a large, rectangular table and filled in my name, address, phone number, height, weight, color of eyes, education, date of birth, mother's place of birth, father's place of birth, my place of birth, and my mother's maiden name. I affirmed that I had never had any disease more serious than chicken pox, that I had never been in prison, and that I had never attempted to overthrow the United States Government.

After this initial step, events moved rapidly. The army must have decided I'd be good for something, because two days later I was notified to report for the written portion of the procedure. This was the Army General Classification Test, commonly referred to as the AGCT, for which it was necessary to achieve a minimum score of 110 for acceptance into the WAAC. Once again, I more than exceeded the minimum requirement, and I received notice to appear for the personal interview.

Until now I had been experiencing only a mild kind of nervousness, but for the personal interview I was genuinely scared. I have always preferred to take fifty written tests rather than face one grim-visaged interviewer. There's something about the self-assurance and the imperturbable calm of sober-faced inquisitors sitting in judgment that frightens me to death. They always look like they hate me.

On the morning of the interview, I was in my room ironing a slip preparatory to getting dressed. I figured that, in my nervousness and distraction, I might get hit by a car en route to the interview, and if *I* was going to be a mess, at least my underwear would be neat.

There was a knock on my door, and in walked my sister, Miriam.

I guess I wasn't too surprised. I had called her several days earlier and had broken the news that I was being processed for the WAAC. Miriam was the oldest of the five siblings, and with thirteen years between us, she had always been very protective — kind of a surrogate mother, even now when she had two daughters of her own.

"Well, hello," I said. "What on earth are you doing here?" I asked innocently, as though I didn't know. I was the baby of the family, and babies don't go to war.

"Oh, I just thought I'd run over and spend the day with you," she answered.

Some run. Ninety miles — by train.

"Oh, good. Glad you came," I lied. I really was in no mood for arguing. "As long as you're here, you can come with me this afternoon."

"Where are you going?"

"For my personal interview for the WAAC."

"As long as I'm here, I'd like to talk to you about that," she said, as if that was not the reason for her visit.

"OK."

"You know, if you feel very strongly about contributing to the war effort, you can do it very effectively without going away from home."

"But I heard you say you thought the WAAC was such a great idea, and if you didn't have your responsibilities at home, you would join."

Suddenly she was deaf.

"You could work with the American Women's Volunteer Service," she said. "At least they won't end up in Germany, Russia, or Algeria with bombs flying all around."

"WAACs aren't going overseas. The nearest I'll get to Germany, Russia, or Algeria will be Georgia, California, or Texas."

"That's today. What makes you so sure the law won't be changed?" (She proved to be so right.)

"Do you know what's bothering you?" I asked my sister. "You don't really believe I might wind up lying on a bloody battlefield mumbling deliriously, 'Water! Water!' or in an enemy camp being tortured every hour on the hour for not revealing the exact moment of the big push. You're afraid there won't be anyone to tell me to wear a heavy scarf in cold weather, or that the army won't bake me a cake on my birthday."

She passed on that one, too.

"You could also be an airplane spotter."

"Oh, sure. I'd probably send the entire Forty-eighth Squadron after a flock of swallows flying to Capistrano."

She didn't give up. She suggested doing USO work, rolling bandages for the Red Cross, knitting sweaters and helmets for the soldiers, and wrapping packages for overseas. She was getting to the bottom of the barrel, but she scraped all the way to the recruiting building and all the time we sat in the anteroom waiting my turn. She was saying something about air raid wardens when my name was called.

I was totally unprepared for the vision that greeted me as I entered the small office. Seated behind a desk was one of the handsomest men I had ever seen. Maybe it was the pipe. I had always had a weakness for a man with a pipe. But he also had dark, wavy hair; big, black, piercing eyes; and matinee idol features. I forgot to be charming; instead I was thinking, "Here is some hunk of man."

If I was nervous before, I was a total wreck now.

"Have a seat, please," said the beautiful head as it motioned to the chair at the side of the desk.

Easy, girl, I said to myself. He may not be as perfect as he looks. Maybe he's only four feet tall and has a fat belly.

Armed with these deprecatory possibilities, I lifted my chin, and, with consummate dignity, I took a step forward.

I still don't know how it happened. But suddenly, with my head leading my body as if I were running interference, I was propelled forward in big leaping steps. Unable to stop myself, on and on I went as though I had been shot out of a cannon, until I landed on my stomach across the desk of the handsome Lieutenant, looking up into his big, black, piercing eyes.

He looked into mine and said, "Whoops."

That's exactly what I thought I would do right then and there — whoops in humiliation and disgust.

"Are you all right?" asked the Lieutenant as he helped me off his desk.

"I'm OK. I'm sorry. I guess I tripped," I said sheepishly as I crept over to the chair. I sat down with my legs slightly apart to make room for the lump that was emerging on the inside of my left leg. By this time, I was thoroughly crushed, but infinitely thankful that I had paid such careful attention to my underwear.

As I glanced at the Lieutenant, I thought for an instant I saw a look of compassion. Maybe it was pity. Anyway, as soon as he began the interview, his face became an unfathomable deadpan.

I was glad I had given some thought to the probable nature of the questions I would be asked. Despite my initial setback and the fuzziness of my brain, I answered with some semblance of lucidity when he asked about my family, what kind of work I thought I would like to do in the WAAC, and why I wanted to join the WAAC.

With each reply, I looked into the Lieutenant's face

for some encouraging acknowledgment that he approved my answer. There was nothing — no visible indication of approval or disapproval — only a statue-like passivity that served to exacerbate my discomfort.

Then suddenly I had the chance to prove myself.

"How," he asked, "would you mete out justice to the Nazi war criminals if you were given that job to do after the war?"

I jumped in with all the vehemence and passion I could muster. My eyes grew fierce, and without hesitating one moment, I spat out, "I'd string them up on the nearest tree."

At last, I had gotten through to him. His eyes opened wide for a moment. Then he closed them, dropped his chin to his chest, and groaned, "Oh, no. You, too?" He looked positively ill when he raised his head and said, "That's all. You may go."

Puzzled, I left the room. Outside the door, as I started to walk away, my head cleared (natch, when else?) and the puzzle unraveled. Into my mind flashed a picture of a jury box, defense attorneys, prosecuting attorneys, and prisoners democratically presented before the bar of justice.

I clapped the palm of my hand against my forehead. Of course! Trial by jury according to the due processes of the democratic law. That was the intelligent answer.

I knew a moment of panic. I looked back at the door and I wanted to run back and say, "Honest, I didn't mean it. I really do know better. Could I please have another chance?"

But I couldn't and I didn't, of course. Instead, now *I* groaned. All the good that had gone before had been undone, and as comic Henry Morgan would have said, "in one swell foop." But what a foop!

"You look terrible. What happened?" asked Miriam.

"I blew it. You can stop worrying. I'll knit sweaters."

But apparently the examiners felt I wouldn't do too much damage to my country, for several days later I received notice to report for my physical examination.

I called Miriam to tell her the news.

"Uh-huh," she said. I still don't know what that meant.

CHAPTER THREE

Bottoms Up

With the written test and the personal interview behind me, my relief was indescribable. A tremendous burden had been lifted from me, and as I walked down the familiar street to the recruiting building, I sang. Ahead of me lay only the physical examination, and I expected it to be a breeze. A doctor would flash a little light into my eyes, my ears, my nose, my throat, I'd say "Ah," and I'd inhale and exhale a few times. I supposed he would listen to my heart too, and I wasn't too thrilled with the prospect of unbuttoning my blouse and baring my chest to a male doctor. This, of course, was before the explosion of nudity on the world scene, and when women's boobs and stuff were considered very private. I anticipated I would be embarrassed and that I would blush a little, but I bolstered my courage by telling myself it would be nothing to speak of, which was just about like my chest anyway.

So, merrily, I made my way down the street warbling in four different keys, Irving Berlin's:
"God bless America,
Land that I love!
Stand beside her, and guide her
Through the night with a light from above."

When I reached the building, I was directed one flight up, first door to the right, and I entered a room about thirty feet square. It was a cold and ugly room with bare wooden floors and no furniture except for long, wooden benches that lined all four walls. Several young ladies were seated on benches in various parts of the room, purses and folded hands in their laps. I assumed they were early for their appointments, because mine was for nine o'clock, and it was only a quarter of nine. I sat down on one of the benches and waited too. Several more women came into the room, nine o'clock came and went, and still I waited. At nine-thirty, there were twenty-five of us, and we all waited. I was getting extremely impatient and was glad that when the doctor arrived, I would be first. I felt sorry for the poor gals who would have to wait for hours.

At long last, a door opened on the opposite side of the room through which I had entered. A woman stepped into the room dressed in a collarless white uniform much like the one worn by hospital workers.

"May I have your attention, please?" she said. "I'm the matron. Please listen carefully and obey all instructions. First answer 'Present' when your name is called."

She called twenty-five names, twenty-five women dutifully called "Present," and the matron said, "Good. Everybody's here. Now get undressed."

Something must be wrong with my hearing. I could have sworn she said, "Get undressed."

"Take everything off," she continued, "dress, stockings, underwear, everything — and I mean everything."

I didn't believe it. Surely I must be dreaming. Get undressed to the skin before twenty-four women I had never seen before in my life? Was she out of her mind?

It wasn't that I was a prude. I had showered in ladies' locker rooms with many other women present, but I had had at least a bobbing acquaintance with the other bare-breasted women. Besides, after taking off my clothes, I'd take a shower — I didn't just stand around in the nude doing nothing. I had also spent summer vacations in places that provided dormitory-type sleeping arrangements, and after taking off my clothes, I'd put on pajamas. But for the life of me, I just couldn't envision anything more inelegant or deflating than standing around bare-assed with twenty-four other bare-assed women with nothing to do.

I know that had I been asked to carry a gun, or to make a parachute jump behind enemy lines, or to volunteer for a suicide mission, I might have balked, coward that I am, but in the end I'd have bitten the bullet and done my duty. This, however, was far above and beyond the call of duty, and I got up to leave.

"Sit down, young lady," said the matron. "I'm not through." I sat.

"After you're undressed, fold up your clothes, so you can carry them with you. I'll be back shortly. Just sit on the benches and wait for me."

Where the hell did she think we'd be going in the nude?

She turned to leave the room, and then she had an afterthought. "You'd better wear your shoes. We don't want you getting splinters in your pretty little feet, now, do we?" And she laughed, "Ha, ha, ha."

Hey, lady, if we're to sit on these benches, what about the splinters in our pretty little behinds? Ha, ha, ha.

As soon as she was gone, I bolted for the door through which I had entered and which led to the stairway and freedom. It was locked!

Slowly, I made my way back to the bench and sat down. I was numb. For the second time that day, a tune entered my head, Daniel Decatur Emmett's:

I wish I were in Dixie,
Away, away.
In Dixieland, I'll take my stand
To live or die in Dixie.
Away, away, away down south in Dixie.
Away, away, away down south in Dixie.

Or away up north in the Yukon, or anywhere but Philadelphia.

I looked around the room and surveyed the scene. Most of the women hadn't moved a muscle. Obviously, this was not an uninhibited group. Again, we must remember that this was long before the explosion of *Hair* and *Oh, Calcutta!* on the American scene; bathers on Fire Island were still wearing something called a bathing suit; and it was probably the year Burt Reynolds was still in the centerfold of a diaper.

Two of the women, however, had obeyed orders and were getting undressed. After a few minutes, some of the other women began going through some motions, probably because they were embarrassed at being embarrassed. One started fumbling with her

hat; another grappled with her earrings; a third dawdled with her shoes, while a fourth diddled with her
stockings. One busy little bee kept taking off her
glasses and putting them back on.

At some point in all of this finagling, we faced the
awful truth. In order to get undressed, we would have
to take off our clothes. So, slowly and reluctantly, they
began to come off — the dresses, the stockings, the
bras, the panties, and finally the last protection against
total nudity, the girdles or corsets, as the casing might
be.

And there we stood, the potential protectors of
American freedom, in all our glorious, eye-filling
splendor — a splendor that knew no grades in Army
General Classification tests nor quality of performance in interviews; there were no strong and no
weak, no brilliant performers to be contrasted with
muttonheads, no high scorers as opposed to just-
passers. Nosiree. Here, in this great leveling room,
there were only the firm and the flabby, the round and
the angular, the concave and the convex, the buxom
and the flat, and last, but by no means least, the
swingers. Yep! There we stood — twenty-five women
— in all our undraped glory, stripped to the buff,
physically and spiritually.

Quickly, I found a partial solution to my discom-
fiture. I sat down on the wooden bench, splinters be
damned; I deposited my clothes in my lap, and I
folded my arms over my chest, concealing all points of
interest.

Some of the women were ingenious in other ways.

For instance, there was the sleeve-dangling strategy. This consisted of crossing the clothes-filled arms over the chest while deftly permitting the sleeves of the dress to dangle downward toward center. There was also the hat-in-hand maneuver. These women held their hats in their hands, casually permitting the hats to dangle downward toward center. (The girls carrying the small pillbox hats that were all the rage that year were out of luck). The gal I liked the best was the one facing the back wall.

Eventually the matron returned. Standing in the doorway, she called out, "Form a single line in front of me. Carry your clothes with you."

I slipped into my shoes, then decided I needed some dignity and put on my hat and gloves.

I scrambled over to where the line was forming, got behind a behind, and listened to the matron.

"In the corridor," she was saying, "are individual examining rooms that are numbered. As we pass each room, I will call the name of the young lady who is to drop off the line and into that room. When you get inside, get on the examining table and cover yourself with the sheet. Now, follow me."

I threw back my bony white shoulders and held my hatted head high. We started marching. The twenty-five pairs of high heels added just the right touch of grandeur to the twenty-five pairs of bouncing buttocks as we paraded from the room.

"Blumenthal — number four," called the matron. I turned into the cubicle. In one sweeping glance, my eyes took in a chair, an examining table, and a sheet. In one sweeping leap, I was on the examining table with my clothes on the chair and the sheet up to my nose. Then I prayed the doctor would be a woman.

Not that I was too thrilled about being examined by a woman doctor, either. In my lifetime, I hadn't had much experience with doctors. The only parts of my body I had ever exposed to any medical person had been my right arm (broken at the age of eight in the school playground) and my left leg (with a hole in the knee from playing, "Red Rover, Red Rover, let Rosie come over," and falling down a broken sewer).

"Good morning," said the man as he entered the room.

"Oh, no! Please go away," I pleaded as I pulled the sheet up over my head.

"Oh, come now," he said as he approached the examining table.

"Are you the doctor?" I asked through the sheet.

"Well, I'm not the firing squad," he answered.

"I think I'd rather you were."

He removed my hat and my shoes, pulled the sheet from my face, and said, "Peek-a-boo." I pulled the sheet up again.

He laughed. I couldn't see him, but I could hear him.

"Now your gloves," he said as he pulled out my hands from behind my back where I had hidden them because I felt I had to keep *something* on.

Then he started the examination. He thumped my chest, punched my stomach, poked my liver, and tickled my ribs — counterclockwise. Then he thumped my vertebrae, punched my sacroiliac, poked me fore, and tickled me aft. Any minute, I expected he would stamp my rump, "Prime — U.S. Government Inspected."

Apparently he was satisfied that I had all the essentials and that all my equipment was in good working order.

"There," he said. "That wasn't so bad, was it?"

"Of course not. Not for you."

"You'll go down the hall now, turn left and go into room twenty-four for a chest x-ray. Here, put this on, and your shoes, too, and leave your clothes here. After you've had your x-ray, you'll come back and get dressed."

With one hand holding the sheet up to my armpits, with the other I took from him what looked like another sheet, and he left. But then I could see this was not another sheet, because it had strings. It was one of those white, shapeless, ugly coveralls presumptuously called a "gown." I was in luck. I found that if I put my hand behind me and pulled the two ends together they almost met — except, that is, when I bent over to put on my shoes. Then my luck bottomed out.

CHAPTER FOUR

Who Said Cows Aren't Purple?

The chest x-ray completed, I was directed to the room next door where a doctor examined my ears, nose, and throat.

"You can go back now and get dressed," he instructed. "Then go to room seventeen for your eye examination."

Holding my handsome white creation together in the back, I flitted happily through the corridors, confident that all would be well. I anticipated no difficulty with this final phase of the examination; I knew my vision was twenty-twenty.

I was right. The eye examination proceeded smoothly. I read the letters on the chart, top to bottom, the eye doctor peered into my eyes with his little searchlight, and it was all over — all the preliminaries for admission to the Women's Army Auxiliary Corps.

I rose from the chair in a state of exhilaration. "Hallelujah!" I exclaimed, smiling at the doctor. "What a relief! It's all over!"

"Sit down there," he said, motioning toward a table. As I sat down, he came toward me carrying a box. It looked like a large cookie box, much larger than family size, and I smiled as I thought how soon I would be seeing army-sized boxes of farina, army-sized pots, pans, cans of vegetables, cans of fruit. Now, out of an army-sized cookie box, I was going to get some cookies. How nice! It had been a long morning and I welcomed some refreshments. I hoped they were fig newtons.

The doctor placed the box in front of me with the words, "Pick out all the red ones and call me when you're through." He walked back to the examining chair to his next patient.

Red cookies? I looked into the large, coverless box and my mouth flew wide open. They weren't cookies at all. Inside the box lay an assortment of small clusters of wool in a variety of vivid colors.

I was stunned. The doctor wanted me to pick, not red cookies, but red clusters of wool from among the orange, green, yellow, purple, blue, magenta, mauve, brown, plum, and bronze.

Gelett Burgess once wrote:
I've never seen a purple cow,
I hope I never see one.
But this I'll tell you anyhow,
I'd rather see than be one.

Well, I'm different. I *have* seen a purple cow — and a turquoise one, and a yellow one, and a red one. I've also seen pink horses, navy-blue bananas, and the orange Mediterranean. I'm color-blind.

Up until this time, I had never attached too much importance to my deficiency. It had been more of a nuisance than a handicap.

In ophthalmological circles, names have been bestowed on various types of color blindness — protanopia for red, deuteranopia for green, Daltonism for red-green. I didn't have the faintest notion of the name given to my particular type of color-blindness. As I continued to stare in numbed horror at the box before me, all I knew was that I wished the eye doctor would go back to his damned ophthalmological circles and leave me in peace. Because, if he didn't, in a very short time, I would be in pieces.

Deep down, I knew, of course, that I was hoping for the impossible. The small, determined jut of his big, fat chin betokened the steadfastness of a man who knew exactly what he wanted and wasn't going to be happy until he got it. Right now, this man wanted red clusters. Boy, was he going to be miserable!

He had instructed me to notify him when I was ready. Well, I was ready right then and there — to end my short-lived army career. From where I sat, it didn't look too promising.

Wouldn't it be nice, I thought, if I could say some magic words that would make the box disappear? Or better yet, the doctor. I tried Abracadababra . . . Vasa Murrhina . . . fine, fine, superfine . . . vamoose. Nothing.

I sat in a state of shocked immobility as the minutes sped away. What should I do — surrender or attack? Should I make a stab at it, and live with the satisfaction that I had gone down fighting? If I didn't try, would I endure sleepless, tormented nights wondering whether I might have succeeded?

Hopefully, I looked into the box. No luck. The wool clusters were still there. A quick glance to my right confirmed that the doctor was too. Well, it was do or die.

I reached in, picked a cluster that looked as though it might be a likely prospect, and held it in front of me. How lucky could I get? Clamped between my thumb and forefinger was a beautiful cluster of wool in a magnificent shade of red. Somebody up there likes me, I thought. I laid the wool on the table next to the box and prepared to reach in for a second cluster. Suddenly, the one on the table turned orange . . . or was it pink? . . . purple? . . . brown? . . . I wished I were dead. I picked up the wool from the table and tried twisting it in front of my eyes, peering here, scrutinizing there, hoping for some magic turn that would reveal a color clearly identifiable as red. I brought it close to my nose and held it at arm's length. I turned it toward the light and bent with it toward the floor. I stuck my neck out to it and pulled my chin away from it. Alas. No twist — no turn — no hopeful gyration revealed any color I could identify with certainty.

While I was toying with the idea of throwing the whole box into the air and going down to defeat in a blaze of flying colors, I became aware of the Major. He was sitting directly opposite me across the three-foot width of the table, leaning back in a swivel chair and holding an open newspaper in front of him. He was apparently out to lunch. I had been so deeply preoccupied with my clusters and my miseries, I hadn't noticed him.

The Major, on the other hand, hadn't passed over me so lightly. Apparently, over the top of his newspaper, he had been watching my confusion. It was his head that first attracted my attention. It was moving slowly from left to right. At first I interpreted the motion as the kind that accompanies incredulity — like, my God, even my three-year-old knows colors. Then, when he repeated the motion from left to right and back and also knitted his brow, I understood. He was vetoing my choice of red!

In a flash, I dropped the cluster of wool, picked another, and held it up. Again the Major's head moved from left to right and back. Quickly, I dropped it and picked up a third. Once more came the negative motion.

Then it happened. With a swift glance in the direction of the examining chair to confirm that the eye doctor's attention was elsewhere, the Major leaned forward and reached over his newspaper. He dipped into the box and pulled out one-two-three-four-five-six magnificent clusters of varying shades of what I assumed were red and dropped them on the table. Then he leaned back in his swivel chair, lifted his newspaper in front of his face, and once again was out to lunch.

It had happened so quickly, I was flabbergasted and didn't know what to do. Yet I knew I couldn't sit there forever doing nothing, and I rationalized that if it was okay with an army officer who wore gold oak leaves on his shoulders, it ought to be okay with me. So, still dazed, I called over to the eye doctor in a very small voice, "I'm ready."

"Very good," said the doctor, viewing my selection. "Now pick yellow." And he was gone.

The Major was tuned in. He leaned forward, dipped again, pulled out six or seven golden clusters, and returned to his newspaper.

"Ready," I called, in a much stronger voice this time. Desperation and the sweet smell of success must have made me an easy convert to a life of crime.

"That's fine," said the doctor. "Now pick blue."

A few more dips by the Major, another commendation by the doctor, and it was all over. I had passed the color test.

As I was leaving the room, I stopped in the doorway, looked back at my benefactor, and threw him an appreciative little wriggle of my fingers. He responded with a big fat wink that clearly said, "Boy, did we screw 'em."

CHAPTER FIVE

Oil, Anyone?

This time the testing was truly finished. I had only to await word of my acceptance or rejection. I thought this might be a matter of weeks, but apparently the army wasn't taking any chances of losing this gem. In two days' time, I was notified to report for swearing in.

Twelve of us stood in line abreast of one another; a Lieutenant Colonel stood before us to administer the oath. When I raised my right hand, it was shaking like a vibrator belt, and my heart was pounding so hard, any moment I expected the Lieutenant Colonel to roar, "Whose heart is that? Knock it off." I hoped he couldn't hear what my heart was saying: "Run — it's not too late! Run — it's not too late!" Then, suddenly, it was. I said "I do," and I was married to Uncle Sam.

"Congratulations," said the Lieutenant Colonel. "It is indeed my pleasure to welcome into the Women's Army Auxiliary Corps the first enlisted women from the Philadelphia area. We know we shall have reason to be proud of you. Now return to your homes and wait for your call to active duty. We don't know exactly when that will be. Be ready."

I arrived back in Paterson, New Jersey, in mid-August. My family was far from happy about the enlistment of their baby, but since it was a fait accompli, they had no choice but to accept it. They offered to help with my preparations — that is, my mother and sisters offered their services, and my brothers offered their wives. However, there wasn't anything anyone could do for me. My chores were such that only I could accomplish them: getting my leave processed, sorting my belongings for saving and discarding, getting the necessities for going away, and then, of course, packing.

I dispatched a letter to the Board of Education requesting a military leave of absence. School was scheduled to reopen on September 9, only three weeks away. My leave was promptly granted by a letter that also confirmed the indefinite date of commencement of leave. I had asked that I be permitted to teach until such time as I received my orders to report for active duty — an arrangement I deemed financially expedient in view of the $21 a month I would earn as a WAAC. I don't suppose the board liked the uncertainty of the date, but it knew better than to tangle with a women's army.

Next, I tackled the nauseating job of sorting my clothing and other personal effects. This doesn't sound like such an unpleasant task, but for me, it's murder. If I have to decide whether to discard a plaid woolen dress I haven't had on my back in four years, or whether there's a remote chance I might wear it to the supermarket on a rainy Thursday, I wind up with frazzled nerves, and the dress winds up back in the closet, where it hangs unworn till the next year when I have to make up my mind whether to discard it or whether there's a remote chance I might wear it to the supermarket on a rainy Thursday.

As it turned out, disposing of the clothing wasn't as bad as I anticipated. My eyes made one loving sweep of the whole collection, and up it went into the attic. (During the four years I was in the service, periodically I would write home and give away certain of my clothing, so by the time I came home, I had none of it left anyway. So much for loving sweeps.) And preparations were made even simpler by a list I had received on the day I was sworn in. It was captioned, "INFORMATION FOR WOMEN'S ARMY AUXILIARY CORPS ENROLLEES REGARDING PERSONAL EQUIPMENT WHICH MAY BE BROUGHT TO THE W.A.A.C. TRAINING CENTER." It read as follows:

Alcohol, rubbing	Cosmetics
Billfold	Cup, eye
Blades	Curlers, hair
Bottle, hot water	Dentifrice
Brush, clothes	Deodorant
Brush, hair	Equipment, athletic
Brush, nails	Floss, dental
Cap, bathing	Hangers, coat
Civilian clothes, 2 outfits	Housecoat, thin material
Cloth, wash	Kit, sewing
Comb	Kit, shoeshine

Knife, pocket	Set, manicure
Lotion, hand	Shorts
Mirror	Slacks
Napkins, sanitary	Slippers, bedroom
Nets, hair	Soap
Pen, fountain	Stamps
Pencil	Stationery
Powder, bath	Suit, bathing
Powder, foot	Tissues, cleansing
Powder, talcum	Tweezers
Razor	Wash, eye
Scissors	Wash, mouth
Shampoo	Watch, wrist

It was a good list. It covered well the situations and eventualities encountered by the female traveler who plans an extended and indefinite stay away from home. Although I can't say I travel often with a knife, pocket (only when I'm planning to eat caramels that will stick to my teeth), or, for that matter, with a cup, eye (only when I'm planning to eat caramels that will stick to my eye). I'd be more apt to carry a brush, tooth, and Aids, Band.

Miriam, at the house one day when I was checking off my list, felt it was not complete. She made an insertion after net, hair: oil, mineral. On a subsequent visit, fearful that I might ignore her suggestion of preparedness, she arrived bearing a fifth of Squibb's M.O.

Three busy weeks went by. I worried — sometimes that the army had forgotten me, and sometimes that it hadn't. In the meantime, I had completed all my preparations. I had partied and said my goodbyes to friends and relatives. My trunk was packed all the way from alcohol, rubbing, down to but not including watch, wrist, which I was planning to wear on my wrist, skinny. In my trunk also were countless going-away presents, including twelve boxes of writing paper, five address books, seven cuticle clippers, and nine boxes of candy.

On Wednesday, September 9, I returned to school. At 6:05 that evening, while I was having dinner, the phone rang.

"Is this Blumenthal's?" a male voice asked.

"Yes, it is," I answered.

"I'd like to speak to Auxiliary Blumenthal."

"Sorry. There's no one here by that name.

"Is your name Rose Blumenthal?"

"Why, yes."

"You're Auxiliary Blumenthal. Report to the Baltimore and Ohio Station, 24th and Chestnut Streets in Philadelphia, not later than 1:15 P.M. on Saturday, September 12. A letter confirming these instructions is in the mail."

CHAPTER SIX

They Never Gave Me A Gardenia

It was the night before my departure. Gathered at my home to bid me farewell were my assorted next of kin and some friends. I had resolved earlier that the evening would not be a sad one. I flitted around the house with snappy witticisms like, "Don't worry, the war will be over soon now that I'm in the army," and "Those Nazis had better watch out, because here I come!" It was a magnificently contrived performance, but it didn't work. Apparently my mother didn't appreciate my flits or my wits. She cried. Then I cried. Then everybody cried.

This hilarious evening was finally over, and I said my watery goodbyes. I descended the stairs amid calls of:

"Take care of yourself!"

"I will!"

"Don't forget to write."

"I won't!"

"Eat everything they give you."

"I will!"

"Don't get court-martialed."

"I won't!"

I was to spend the night in Nutley at Miriam's home; then she, her husband, and her two daughters were to drive me to Philadelphia to entrain.

When I climbed into the car the following morning, I felt my throat constrict. At this last moment, I was feeling emotional beyond measure: for my family; for my friends; for poor, dear eighth-grader Anthony, who couldn't do long division by three numbers; and for my magnificent new tailored powder-blue suit, which I loved with an undying passion and which I knew, somehow, I would never wear again.

We arrived at the Baltimore and Ohio railroad station in Philadelphia about 12:30 and walked into a waiting room seething with wartime bedlam. Soldiers and civilians occupied virtually every inch of space. It was practically impossible to cover ground without pushing or being pushed. Our search for the WAAC group was complicated by soldiers not yet in uniform who were scheduled to entrain on this day also. So all over the place, women were clinging to men and men were clinging to women, and it was impossible to tell which were going and which were staying.

We had already covered the full length of the station and were getting ready to blaze a new trail, when we spotted a group that seemed engaged in an unusual frenzy of activity. We pushed closer and saw women wearing gardenias, photographers madly taking pictures of the women, and reporters interviewing and making notes in their little black books.

I stepped into the sphere of action and was pounced upon by a reporter. When I confirmed that, yes, I was a WAAC, be began to interview me. My responses didn't send him scooting off to phone his scoop to his newspaper, but the *Philadelphia Inquirer* did print, "Miss Rose Blumenthal, attractive in her tailored suit, and an eighth-grade schoolteacher, said, 'My students told me to kill a couple of Japs.'" A friend sent me the clipping, and I was thrilled indeed. It wasn't a world-shaking statement, to be sure, but it was the first time I had ever been quoted in a newspaper. Also the last.

A voice boomed through the microphone: "All WAACs over here, please." A Sergeant called the roll from a list on his clipboard, did an about face, saluted a Lieutenant Colonel, and said, "All WAACs present and accounted for, sir."

The Lieutenant Colonel stepped forward and stood before us. "This is an auspicious occasion," he said. "We're proud of you. You are making many sacrifices in joining the Women's Army Auxiliary Corps — leaving comfortable homes, secure jobs, beloved family and friends, to enter into a new life which will make many demands upon you. Yet you do so willingly because your country needs you." There was more in this vein; in fact, this farewell speech was so stirring I was eager to rush off and enlist, until I remembered I already had.

This last parting was the worst. I could hardly believe that after all the weeks of decision-making, processing, and preparing, the moment had actually arrived for making the final break between my secure life as a civilian and my uncertain life as a WAAC. Lest the folks notice my emotion, I quickly deposited four abbreviated kisses, and, my farewells and my bridges behind me, I hurried off to Track B to join the procession already filing through the gate.

Only later did I realize they had never given me a gardenia.

Clutching my overnight case and my handbag (my trunk had been sent on ahead), I boarded the train. I was looking forward to a window seat where I could watch, with deepening nostalgia, the charming hamlets go whizzing by, and see, with heaviness of heart, the lovely quaint towns I was leaving behind, the same charming hamlets and the same quaint towns that only yesterday I had called one-horse whistlestops. But apparently other women had the same idea, and by the time I boarded the train, there wasn't a window seat left. Then, as though my cup of sorrows was not sufficiently full, I chose to share a seat with a tall, dark, attractive young lady by the name of Janet who, it turned out, had only the night before dated a gentleman friend of mine in Philadelphia.

I wished desperately I could go into the club car and drown my sorrows in my usual Manhattan — three parts vermouth, two parts rye. But instructions had been explicit: no hard liquor en route. So the best I could manage was to drown my mounting sorrows in three parts seltzer and two parts chocolate syrup.

With not too much to do at first except talk to Janet, whom I already despised passionately, I sat back and concentrated on appraising my trainmates, some

of whom would be my companions and bunkmates
for the next four weeks at Fort Des Moines. They were
a heterogeneous group, naturally, as most armies are.
There were tall girls and short ones, skinny ones and
fat ones, young and old, good-looking and bad-
looking. There were Jeannies with light brown hair,
and Idas sweet as apple cider; there were sewing
machine Berthas, riveting Rosies, Edies who were
ladies, and a Tallulah.

It was inevitable that before long conversations
would start throughout the car. How long can you sit
with fangs bared? We pushed back seats, sat in groups,
and talked about the army, naturally, and it was
amazing how much everyone knew. I learned that
failure to keep shoes shined to a mirrorlike gleam was
punishable by a general court-martial, which was the
worst kind; and that if an enlisted person fraternized
with an officer, the punishment was death — for the
enlisted person, of course. My contribution was, "Everybody to the bathroom!" (I hadn't quite gotten used
to "latrines.")

Despite these shocking announcements, we sang
songs. That is, everybody else sang while I, in my usual
fashion, tried, and we had an exciting day. By bedtime,
we were glad to climb into our berths — one in an
upper, two to a lower.

The second day passed very much like the first.
There were no murders — not even any hair pulling
— and we arrived in the city of Des Moines at ten
o'clock in the evening of the thirteenth of September,
tired and disheveled, but by now happy and stimulated.

When, in my fashionable suit with the matching hat, I was herded into an army truck that looked like a covered wagon with a motor, my euphoria abated noticeably. If I were going to be genuinely honest, I would have to admit I was even somewhat appalled. But not nearly so appalled as the gals with the Christian Dior originals and the mink stoles. They damn near fainted.

CHAPTER SEVEN

Never, Never Be Caught With Your Lashes Down

As the truck proceeded toward the WAAC section, its dark walls prevented my seeing any of old Fort Des Moines. Barracks for the WAACs were being constructed on a huge, sandy tract outside the main post, and it was to this extension of Fort Des Moines that we were being driven.

When the truck stopped, two soldiers stood at the back to help us jump out, because obviously our civilian clothes didn't lend themselves to jumping. I saw an area lit by bare electric bulbs on the outside of three two-storied buildings, each with an outside wooden stairway. Across a fifty-foot stretch of dirt, gravel, and sparsely sprouted grass was a low one-story structure that looked like the administration building for the company. In the center of the illuminated clearing were two tables. The larger one was piled high with bed linens and towels. Behind the smaller sat a WAAC Third Officer.

"Line up in single file in front of my table," she ordered. "As you step up to the table, give me your name and your army serial number. Then take two sheets, one pillowcase, and three towels, and go immediately to the barracks and to the bed to which I assign you. The building on the extreme left behind me is number one and will house the first platoon. The middle building will be the second platoon, and that one," she said, pointing to the building on her right, "is platoon number three. The rest of our company arrived earlier today, and you will find other auxiliaries in the barracks when you get there. On the beds, you will find blankets and pillows. Get ready for bed immediately. 'Lights out' will be called soon after we have assigned the last young lady."

My turn came and I said, "Rose Blumenthal, A304062."

"First platoon, second floor, fourth bed on the left."

After picking up my towels and linens, I crossed over to the first building and walked up the outside stairway. Standing in the doorway, I looked into the room and went into shock. Weeks of palliative assurances hadn't prepared me for coming face to face with living by the dozen — two dozen plus one, to be exact, and it totaled four dozen plus two if you counted the twenty-five women on the first floor who would share the latrines. I also observed, with a deep sensation of nausea, the faultlessly aligned beds, the faultlessly aligned footlockers at the foot of the beds, the faultlessly aligned wall lockers. If these were harbingers of the exactitude I would be expected to attain, brother, was I in big trouble! Meticulous housekeeping was not one of my virtues. I was quick to note something else. There wasn't the tiniest pigeonhole where a gal could sneak away for a few moments of quiet reading or a few moments of quiet tears, whichever the occasion demanded.

Earlier arrivals had already settled into activities I would soon recognize as part of the pattern of barracks living. Dressed in pajamas, propped against pillows or sitting on the edges of the beds, they were putting their hair up in curlers and talking, filing their nails and talking, rubbing cold cream into their faces and talking, writing letters and talking, or just talking. One forward-looking lass was wearing earmuffs while reading. I thought quickly, and, in a flash, I galloped over to her, and as best I could with my linen-and-towel-laden hands, I nudged her. She looked up and lifted one earmuff.

"Hi," I said. "I'm Rose. Would you like to trade your earmuffs?"

"For what?" she asked.

"A bottle of mineral oil?"

"No, thanks," she answered. She let the earmuff drop back and continued reading.

Some of the women called friendly welcomes, and I felt better. I prepared my bed as quickly as I could, donned my pajamas, and, towel and toothbrush in hand, hurried to the back of the squadroom and down the inside staircase that led to the latrines. I took a quick look and breathed a sigh of relief. I had found the place for private reading, private crying, and other private activities. The stalls had doors.

Rushing upstairs, I met several of the women from the train rushing downstairs, and, by this time slightly unhinged, we shrieked as though we had been friends since the age of two and hadn't seen each other all that time, and then the rushing continued — some up, some down.

A whistle blew loud and shrill, followed by a voice that called out loud and shrill, "LIGHTS OUT!" The young lady nearest the light switch flipped it, and the room was dark and quiet.

I was overstimulated, and sleep didn't come easily. The unfamiliar mattress was partly to blame. Not that it was so different from my mattress at home, which also abruptly dumped in various places. But after many years of accommodating my body, at least it dumped where I bumped, and that can make all the difference in the world.

I tossed for a while but eventually fell asleep. I dreamed I was in the middle of the parade ground, and Colonel Don Faith, the Commandant of Fort Des Moines, was preparing to pin a Silver Star on my aqua-and-brown-plaid suit for my gallantry in action, when suddenly I awoke with a start. At first I thought I had dreamed the wail that awakened me, but then it wailed again — like a banshee. It was coming from my roommate across the aisle and three beds to the right. Now, this was one contingency I hadn't considered. What was the proper etiquette in such a situation? I was willing to bet even Emily Post wouldn't know.

Now, mind you, it's not that I'm excessively sensitive to sounds when I sleep. I've been known to sleep through the ringing of an alarm clock next to my bed, fire engines racing past my window, and the midnight howling of a cat on the prowl. But they're different. They permeate the subconscious and they're gone (especially if the cat finds another cat). But a snorer is an insidious thing. Snorers lie in wait until their victims have been lulled into unsuspecting serenity, and then they pounce. Snorers penetrate the marrow of the bone; they set every muscle aquiver; they invade the entire being until every nerve fiber is ready to scream, "Roll over!"

If I were going to get any sleep that night, I would have to stop the banshee. I got out of bed, tiptoed over to her corner, took hold of her shoulder gently, and shook her lightly. She jumped, lifted her head and asked, "Wassamatter?"

"Sh-h-h. I'm sorry. Roll over."

"Oh. Sorry." Her head fell back on her pillow, and I went back to bed.

Colonel Faith continued toward me and had just lifted his arms to begin the pinning when I was awakened by the rapid repeat of rifle fire. It was a variation on the snoring theme from my roommate across the aisle and three beds to the left. I got out of bed again, made my way quietly over to the rifles, and put an end to that attack.

I was destined never to get that darned medal. The rifle fire was followed by the chug-chug of a locomotive, a volley of thunder, the hiss of a fiery volcano, the low mooing of a cow in iambic tetrameter. I dashed madly from the chug to the volley to the hiss to the moo, but I had no luck halting the wild cacophony. All I got for my trouble was a mess of splinters and three stubbed toes. Exhausted, frustrated, miserable, and lame, I was forced to admit failure. I resigned myself to the possibility that I might not get a wink of sleep for the duration. But only minutes later, a whistle blew in my ear, a voice bellowed "EVERYBODY UP!" and I awoke.

Thoroughly startled, I sat up. "What's the matter? Is there a fire?" I called out.

Someone flipped the light switch, and the lights went on. "Come on," said a neighbor, "it's time for our first meal at dear old Fort Des Moines."

What a nice army. A midnight snack. But I decided to forego the pleasure. "I'll wait for breakfast," I said, flopping back on my pillow.

"This *is* breakfast," said the neighbor.

"Breakfast? It's pitch dark! What time is it?"

"A quarter to six."

"You're kidding."

"I'm not kidding. You'd better get up."

"A quarter to six! What do they think I am — a chicken?"

Tactfully, she didn't answer.

I sat up and let my legs dangle over the side of the bed. That way they matched my head. Several minutes passed before I could focus my eyes sufficiently to witness the unbelievable chaos I was hearing. There were women, women, women all over the place in various stages of dress and undress. They were scurrying downstairs for speedy showers, and they were scurrying upstairs after speedy showers. I heard anguished cries of "My gosh, where's my slip?" and "Help me yank up my girdle, will you? I'm still damp." I watched them as they fell over footlockers. I watched them as they fell over beds. I watched them as they tumbled over each other in their mad scramble to be ready in the allotted half hour.

I had no choice but to participate in this total madness, and scurrying, scrambling, and tumbling along with the rest, I managed to be showered and dressed with five minutes to spare before whistle time. I tore downstairs to avail myself of one of the large mirrors in the latrine for a hasty makeup job. The mirrors were all taken, and that was no surprise. But the detailed operations in which the damsels in front of them were engaged astonished me. I'm sure, like the rest of us, they were prepared to make many sacrifices, but giving up makeup, apparently, was not one of them. I for one was delighted to have time for powder and lipstick. They, on the other hand, left no makeup detail undone. With meticulous care and expert aim, they stroked the eyebrows, they brushed the eye shadow, they delineated the edges of the eyelids, they curled the lashes. Never, no never, would these women be caught with their lashes down.

Standing on tiptoe, I stretched my neck over a head, dabbed on my lipstick, and dashed upstairs with three other WAACs hot on my tail. A few seconds later, a Third Officer appeared in the doorway and called,

"Atten-HUT!" We didn't know how to stand at "Atten-HUT," but we tried. I doubt we looked much like soldiers, what with the civilian clothes, the rounded shoulders, the sagging stomachs and chins to match — probably more like marshmallows on a stick suffering from sunstroke.

"FALL OUT!" roared the Third Officer.

Now that, we could do. And, oh boy, did we! We fell out and right down the outside stairway and on top of the women rushing from the downstairs squad-room into the Iowa darkness.

By the time we top gals had removed ourselves from the bottom gals and were able to stand up, my eyes had become a wee bit accustomed to the darkness. I could see shapes of women dashing about like football players in a scrimmage. I was licking my wounds when, from somewhere, a voice boomed, "FALL IN!"

I started back toward the barracks. Suddenly I collided with a shape that whispered, "Where are you going?"

"Back to the barracks."

"You can't do that. You'll get in trouble."

"She said 'Fall in,' didn't she? That means go back to bed!"

"That means you have to get in formation here in front of the barracks."

"It does? Then why doesn't she say so?"

I could make out the outlines of the three platoons, one in front of each of the buildings. They were probably the unlikeliest-looking military formations ever formed in the history of warfare. We marched, and I use the term loosely, the fifty yards to the mess hall, aptly named for this military mess clicking toward its portals. At the entrance, we were given the commands to break ranks and enter. Our ranks were already so broken, we had only to enter.

CHAPTER EIGHT

You're Not Supposed To Think In The Army

The mess hall was designed to feed two companies of WAACs, one on each side of the four giant washtubs and the three giant garbage cans that formed a row down the middle of the room. Three rows containing five parallel tables were aligned (faultlessly) on each side. The rectangular wooden tables with benches attached seated five on each side for a total of ten to a table, and for a total accommodation of three hundred enlisted women in the mess hall. Across the back of the room and running its entire width was the service counter, behind which stood the giant stoves, giant pots, giant pans, ladles, mixing spoons, serving spoons, and other miscellaneous giant equipment. Behind this galaxy of oversized accoutrements stood an incongruous quartet — four normal-sized cooks.

We were led in single file past the rows of wooden tables to the counter at the back. Here we picked up our eating utensils and trays, which we moved along the counter to receive the food from the two cooks designated to serve our company. I was in the habit of having nothing more than juice, toast, and coffee for breakfast; but, with no opportunity to snack the night before and having eaten nothing since supper (civilian dinner), I was looking forward to having a bigger-than-usual breakfast. I asked for the stewed peaches, the pancakes, the omelet, the bread and butter, and coffee. (I skipped the farina, a food I had always thought yucky; coming out of the cannibal-like caul-drons, it was even yuckier).

I returned to my table and began to eat. I got no farther than one peach down with four to go when I had to stop. I had begun to get a headache. Going simultaneously were the clankety-clank of 300 metal trays, the clinkety-clink of 300 metal forks, the clon-kety-clonk of 300 metal spoons, the yackety-yack of 300 big mouths, and the beat-beat-beat of one giant tomtom, which had started out as a normal-sized head. You had to be there to appreciate this head-splitting, ear-rending racket. I tried shutting it out by concentrating on the memory of the serenity of my breakfasts at home with just a few of us in the nice, small kitchen, still half asleep, sitting around a nice, small table, with nobody talking to anybody. But each time I thought I had succeeded in capturing those nostalgic moments, cuh-rash! went another tray to the floor. The din became so intolerable that, with most of my food untouched, I escaped from the mess hall and out into the dawn that was just beginning to break over Fort Des Moines.

My psyche being in no condition for more jabbering females for a while, I went for a short walk across the company area to a road on the other side of it where, as far as I could see, were WAAC barracks in various stages of construction to which future WAACs would be brought as soon as a unit was completed. By the time I returned to the squadroom, most of the girls were back from the mess hall and were sitting around and — yep — talking. Except for a few showoffs who were making their beds.

I thought I should get to know my neighbors, so I sat down on my footlocker and started to talk to Barbara on my right. She seemed cold and unresponsive, so I turned to Trudy, on my left. She was from Georgia, and she was blonde and pretty. I should have hated her instantly, but I didn't. She was warm and friendly, and I liked her. She told me she had several reasons for joining the WAAC. For one thing, Trudy was a secretary, so for her the WAAC was an escape from a spreading affliction known as sititus. Besides, she was engaged to a Corporal who was overseas, and Trudy was hopeful she would be sent over too.

"Even if they do change the laws and send WAACs abroad, overseas is an awfully big place," I reminded her.

"I know," she said, "but you never can tell. Strange things do happen," and she related to me the story of the two brothers, who, unbeknownst to each other, were stationed a mile apart, and met when they began to talk through a partition in a field latrine.

"Well, I hope you do better," I said.

We continued to talk for about fifteen minutes,

during which time I told Trudy a little about myself. Then, remembering the condition of my overnight bag, I decided it might be a good idea to get it into some kind of order for easy access to much-used items.

"Why bother?" Trudy asked. "Everything's going into our footlockers and wall lockers pretty soon anyway."

"I know, and it's not that I'm a stickler for neatness, believe me. But my bag looks like a bargain counter in Macy's at the end of a sale day. If I should have to find something in a hurry, I'll be in trouble. I just want to put a few things where I can lay my hands on them. It was nice talking to you. I'll see you around."

"That's one thing you can bet on," said Trudy.

I pulled my bag from under the bed and opened it. It was truly a shambles, the consequence of my frenetic search for my toothbrush in the wee hours of the morning.

Now, let's see. I'll put my toothbrush where I can get at it quickly . . . where is it . . . ah . . . here it is . . . it goes right in this pocket . . . and my toothpaste . . . right here with my toothbrush . . . my hairbrush right here on top of . . .

A whistle blew, and from outdoors a female voice penetrated the squadroom. "FALL OUT!" it barked.

They want us outside. OK, I'll be through in a few minutes.

My comb can go right here . . . and . . . now, let's see . . . where's my shower cap? . . .

"BLUMENTHAL!" a voice boomed into the barracks. It was a male voice.

I jumped. It was only natural that I should jump, since I *was* Blumenthal, but I was also startled at this male intrusion into our no-man's-land. What on earth was a man doing here, and what did he want of me?

I looked around the barracks. How strange. There wasn't a soul in it except me. Where had everybody gone? Sure, I had heard some people rushing out when the whistle blew, but there were always some eager beavers. Where was everybody else?

"BLU-MEN-THAL!"

I flew out to the top of the outside stairway and looked down to the ground below. In the middle of the clearing was a group of women. In the center, the bars on his shoulders gleaming in the morning sun, stood a male officer. All eyes were turned up at me.

"FRONT AND CENTER! ON THE DOUBLE!" roared the officer.

I scooted down the stairs as fast as my three-inch spikes would carry me, lest his nervous system get more nervous. I sprinted across the sandy, pebbled ground, the hairpins flying from my fast-graying upsweep. As I neared the group, the women parted to make a path for my approach to the Lieutenant.

"WHY DIDN'T YOU GET HERE WITH THE REST OF YOUR PLATOON?" he bellowed.

Embarrassed at being singled out for chastisement before an audience of my peers, I began to stutter. "W-well, uh, I was in the middle of . . ." And then I stood speechless with my mouth wide open, staring at the Lieutenant in horrified disbelief. It couldn't be. I must be dreaming. For standing before me and waiting for an answer was my Philadelphia Lieutenant — none other than the one whose office I had entered like Joe DiMaggio sliding into third base.

"Well?" asked the Lieutenant, waiting. There was no sign of recognition on his face.

"Uh — I — uh — "

"There are no excuses in the army!"

"Y-yes, sir. But I thought . . ."

"You're not supposed to think in the army!"

"N-n-no, sir."

"You get here on the double next time. Is that clear?"

Indeed it was. What was even clearer was that I was so mortified by the public rebuke I wanted to die. What the hell could have possessed me? I had actually gone out of my way to expose myself to such indignities: being addressed by my last name without the benefit of a handle, being ordered around as if I hadn't been a schoolteacher. Why in heaven's name hadn't I listened to my sister? Had I stayed at home and rolled bandages for the Red Cross, I would have been treated with the respect due me and enjoyed privacy in the john besides.

I hurried toward Trudy, who was motioning to me to join her. On orders from the Lieutenant, we formed a double line for the purpose of proceeding to the warehouse for the issuance of uniforms.

"What happened to you?" whispered Trudy. "I thought you were right behind me."

"I didn't know it was urgent," I whispered back.

"Are you kidding? In the army, everything is urgent.

When you hear a whistle, you drop everything and run. You did it this morning."

"I didn't know it meant all the time."

"Well, it does."

"Now you tell me."

"I thought everybody knew that."

"Apparently everybody did, except me. Oh, dear Lord, if you have mercy, send me back to New Jercey."

"Your rhyme is OK, but your state's a little off."

"My state's a lot off. I'm in a state of depression from which I doubt I shall ever emerge. You know, somewhere on the post, there's a cannon. I heard it this morning. Now, if I'm in it when it's fired tomorrow morning, I could be in Outer Mongolia by nightfall."

"Oh, come on, don't take it so seriously. You'll be laughing about it tomorrow."

"I doubt it. The way things are going, I may well be drummed out of the Corps by tomorrow."

"Stop worrying. Just don't let it happen again."

"I don't seem to have much choice where that man's concerned. He gets in my way."

"That man is Lieutenant Sommers. He introduced himself before you joined us, right before he called the roll."

"Well, he's trouble for me," I said, and I described to Trudy what had happened in Philadelphia.

"What's he doing here anyway? asked Trudy.

"Probably relieving a WAAC for active duty."

"Hey, that would be a twist, wouldn't it?"

"I read in the paper that male officers would be assigned to all WAAC companies in the beginning, because WAAC officers are fresh out of OCS and need help."

"Well, just forget the whole thing. He'll probably never bother you again."

"Wanna bet?"

"BLUMENTHAL! IS THAT YOU TALKING?"

I shut up, and we entered the warehouse.

Even though it was September, with the exception of heavy, four-buckle Arctic galoshes, we were given summer wear. Our first government issue was as follows:

Raincoat, WAAC	1
Coat, WAAC, summer	1
Skirt, WAAC, summer	2
Waist, WAAC	5
Brassiere, WAAC	2
Girdle, WAAC	1
Pajamas, WAAC, summer	2
Panties, WAAC, rayon	4
Slip, WAAC	3
Stockings, WAAC, anklet	2
Stockings, WAAC, cotton	4
Stockings, WAAC, rayon	4
Hat, WAAC, summer	1
Neckties, WAAC	2
Overshoes, galoshes	1
Shoes, WAAC, athletic	1
Shoes, WAAC, service	2
Bathrobe, WAAC, summer	1
Brush, tooth	1
Gloves, WAAC, dress, cotton	1

Comb, rubber, hard	1
Suit, exercise, WAAC	1
Bag, barrack	2
Insignia, cap, WAAC	1
Insignia, collar, EM, "US"	1
Insignia, collar, Pallas Athene	1

The coat, WAAC, summer, was actually the jacket of the uniform and was referred to in the army as the blouse. Made of khaki chino, it reached below the hip and was belted, making short women look shorter and fat women look fatter, and fat, short women look shorter and fatter. The skirt, WAAC, summer, was of the same material and was straight and narrow, which looked simply marvelous on the women who were straight and narrow. The waist, WAAC, was the shirt under whose collar would go that thingamadoodle called the necktie, WAAC.

We hurried back to the barracks. How eagerly we contemplated putting on our uniforms for the first time! Momentarily, I could even forget the earlier unpleasantness.

All my government issue lay on my unmade bed — the skirt, the blouse, and the shirts to one side; the underwear in a pile in the middle; and the multitude of miscellaneous items scattered on various parts of the bed. Looking over the array of GI toggery, I realized something for the first time: everything that was to go on our bodies was of the same color. Even I, since birth a victim of xanthocynopia, tritanopia, or whateveranopia, could see that the entire clothing issue was khaki — not only the outer garments, the blouse, skirt, shirt, and hat; but also the stockings, the slips, and the panties. And then, just so the monochromatic color scheme would not be disturbed, the khaki bras and the khaki girdles. I thought I would be sick.

Because we had no choice but to put on GIs, we started. First, there was the girdle. As I looked around the room, I could see that the two-way stretches didn't stretch high enough in some cases and stretched too high in others, and not by the wildest stretch of the imagination or the girdle could a body possibly derive one iota of benefit from this piece of GI apparel. But they did serve the purpose of holding up the stockings, and in those cases where women were concave where they should have been convex, the stockings held up the girdle, so it wasn't a total loss.

Then there was the bra. I remembered, nostalgically, that in a long-since-gone other world, I had tried on two dozen different styles before selecting the one whose fit was meticulously enchanting. These GI bras were meticulously all-of-the-same style. What we didn't know at that time was that the once-a-week personal inspection did not include a peek down the bosom. We only knew we had to obey orders, and our orders had been to put on everything GI — inside and outside. So, obediently, we put on the GI bras, and some women were inside and some were outside.

Parting with the pink panties with the two-inch lace — ah! that was the wrench. Especially because, in their place, we had these panties that weren't panties at all. They were drawers — ugly brownish rayon knee-reaching, skin-clinging, low-hanging drawers.

Although, to be entirely fair, I would have to concede that not all the drawers clung and hung low. Some bagged and hung low. I looked around the room at the ludicrous scene of twenty-five women in twenty-five pairs of mud-colored drawers, and I wanted to laugh. Then I looked at my own mud-colored drawers, and I wanted to cry.

Mary Sue, a petite, vivacious brunette formerly of Alabama and presently from across the aisle and two beds north, conscripted two confreres, and, in the middle of the room, in bra, girdle, panties, and stockings, with arms entwined, they kicked and danced chorus-girl fashion, while Mary Sue chanted rhythmically:

"We ah the gals of the Fote de Moines follies,
Also known as GI dollies.
We sing, we dance, and we'll face owah foes
In burstin' bras and droopin' dro'es."

There was still the full-length slip. Now, every woman knows that a full-length slip should be neither full nor flattening but should mold gently over the bosom and then glide gracefully over the hips to form a smooth foundation for the outer garments. The most we could say for the GI slips was that they were matching sets with the drawers — ugly, brown, and sleazy. Their only virtue was that they did cover the drawers. But they also covered our last vestiges of femininity. They were straight from top to bottom, defeating the entire purpose of the bras underneath — that is, had the bras been serving any purpose.

That night I dreamed I went dancing in my GI

underwear and a USO hostess asked, "Care to dance, sir?"

I was aware that the WAAC uniform had been designed by Dorothy Shaver, vice-president of Lord & Taylor. But, oh, dear Lord, forgive me, I can't shake this horrible suspicion that the tailor who made the WAAC underwear might have been the vice president of Wallachs Men's Division.

I think the shoes were the biggest shocker. Most of us were accustomed to wearing those trim little pumps with high heels that clicked along the sidewalk as we walked. The flat-heeled, heavy brown (what else?) oxfords they gave us were gruesome twosomes that anybody under ninety wouldn't be caught dead in at home.

After the fumbling manipulations with the necktie, we put on the rest of the uniform, complete with the insignia — Pallas Athene, goddess of war — and including the Foreign Legion-type kepi. Dressed at last in the uniform of our country, we were proud — indeed, so proud that, with only ten minutes left before whistle time, we did what any red-blooded WAAC would do: We tore outside and took pictures.

CHAPTER NINE

Milton, You Lost
A Customer

It was chow time again. I can't say I was all agog in anticipation of a second exposure to the deafening delights of army mess. Surprisingly, however, dinner (civilian lunch) turned out to be less noisy. I don't mean there was less noise, mind you. The spoons and the forks and the knives and the trays were still clunking and clinking and clonking and clanking and the mouths were still yakking. But I clearly was aware of a significant fact: unless this half-famished body received some life-sustaining nourishment, one un-happy day a connected stack of bones would slip through the shower drain and float through the sewers of Des Moines, Iowa, never to be heard from again. With this in mind, I employed a small psychological exercise called "The Power of Positive Thinking." All the way to the mess hall that noon, I said to myself, "There is NO noise in the mess hall. There is NO noise in the mess hall." Miraculously, it worked. The huge wads of cotton stuffed in my ears helped too.

This time I ate. I had vegetable soup, beef stew, two

potato pancakes, fruit salad, bread and butter, chocolate cake, and coffee. Maybe it was because by this time
I was ravenous, but it didn't matter: every mouthful
tasted delicious. The beef stew was not exactly in the
same class with tornedos sauteed with foie gras, but
neither was it chipped beef on toast, commonly referred to in the army as something-or-other on a
shingle.

After dinner, I took a short walk again in the
company area and then returned to the barracks to
write some letters. I had gotten as far as "Dear Mom"
when a female voice I was beginning to recognize
called "Atten-HUT!" My fountain pen clutched in one
hand and my writing pad in the other, I was off my bed
and on my feet quicker than you could say Lieutenant
Sommers.

Standing inside the doorway was a WAAC officer
— the one who had been popping in and out of our
squadroom since the night before and keeping us on
the run. She introduced herself as Lieutenant Bolton,
our Platoon Commander, and told us we could sit
while she talked to us.

Lieutenant Bolton was an extremely good-looking
young woman, about thirty, with a sweet face and a
shy smile. Her dark hair was swept back softly over
her ears to form a bun at the back of her head. She had
even features and beautiful teeth, and when she spoke,
her voice was soft and whispery. It seemed anomalous
that this gentle, kind-looking person could discharge
the harsh commands we had been hearing. She
looked as though she should be whispering reference

numbers to teenagers in a public library instead of barking orders to women in an army squadroom. I wondered about her: what had motivated her to join the WAAC? What kind of work had she done as a civilian? Were her drawers brown and droopy like mine?

Lieutenant Bolton explained that she was one of three Platoon Commanders assigned to Company Eight, Third Regiment. Lieutenant Sherman, who was presently our Acting Company Commander, would be the WAAC Company Commander after a "breaking in" period. Until then, our Company Commander would be Lieutenant Peter Sommers. Oh, goody!

She thought there might be some confusion in our minds about the rank titles we had been hearing. She explained that officially WAAC officer ranks were Third Officer, Second Officer, and First Officer, equivalent to Second Lieutenant, First Lieutenant, and Captain. WAAC officers wore the same rank insignia as army officers, however, and, as a result, were usually addressed the same way.

Now it was time for some army orientation. This would be our first formal indoctrination into the ways of the army, and from this moment on, infractions would not be dealt with lightly. We learned that:
- The first person to see an officer approaching must call out, "Attention!"
- Retreat, which signaled the end of the working day, was at five o'clock.
- "Lights out" was at nine o'clock.

- Bed check was at eleven o'clock, and you'd better be there.
- From noon on Saturday until reveille Monday morning, we were free to go and do as we pleased.
- We could go to Bessie's Beauty Parlor right outside the main gate any time from noon on Saturday until reveille Monday.
- After smoking outdoors, we were to roll the wrapper of the cigarette into a minuscule ball, and waft it, together with the tobacco, to the winds. (The first time I tried this I was walking with Trudy. The timing was unfortunate. She was talking, I was wafting, and a north wind was blowing. Result: the tobacco wafted right into Trudy's mouth. I tried to mollify her by pointing out that for the price of one cigarette, we could have two miserable habits: I could smoke and she could chew. She thanked me but declared she preferred to pick her own miserable habits).

The army orientation was followed by instructions on the arrangement of a footlocker. Trudy was right. I shouldn't have bothered straightening the mess in my overnight bag, especially in view of the dire consequences.

We gathered round a footlocker that Lieutenant Bolton selected at random, and she instructed its owner to hand her specific items as she asked for them. She talked as she demonstrated.

"First, keep in mind that only government issue goes into the footlocker — that and nothing else. It goes like this." As she asked for and was handed an item, she put it in its place as follows:

Bottom section: pajamas, front right; slips, front left; panties, back right; stockings, back left; girdles, front and center.

Top tray, front section, right to left: toothbrush, toothpaste, comb, brush, cosmetics bag, washcloth, clothes brush, hand lotion, shampoo.

Top tray, back section, right to left: sewing kit, pocket knife, bath powder, foot powder, ad infinitum — and heaven and the Commanding General help anyone who dared deviate from this arrangement.

Frankly, I was revolted. This was exactly what my sister Anne's dresser drawers looked like. Some of the items were different, true, but the fastidiously precise arrangement was disgustingly familiar: each separate item in its separate place with nowhere the suggestion of a wrinkle or a departure from strict alignment. I could still hear my mother: "Why can't you keep your things like your sister does? When I look in her dresser, it's such a pleasure."

How to make an army bed came next. The Lieutenant walked over to one of the beds, and we crowded around. I jostled myself into a choice viewing spot, not because I cared that much, but because I was well aware of my accomplishments as a homemaker, and I knew that in my own best interests I had better not miss a move.

First, she ripped off the sheets and the blanket and deposited them on the footlocker. So far, so good. I could do step number one without any problems.

Even when she spread the sheet and tucked the two ends neatly under the mattress, I was able to follow with a minimum of difficulty. It was during the next operation she lost me. At the side of the bed, several inches from the foot, she lifted the edge of the sheet with her left hand. Then she tucked it under the mattress with her right hand. Then she pulled with her left, pushed with her right, yanked with her left, smoothed with her right, jabbed with her left, hooked with her right, and presto! she had a magnificent corner — neat, square, and sharp. Then she went to the other side of the bed. She lifted, she pulled, she tucked, she yanked, she smoothed, she jabbed, and she hooked, and lo! there was another breathtaking sight of incomparable beauty. By the time she had completed the four square corners, spread the top sheet, and laid the blanket (khaki) over it and pulled it taut, I was utterly and totally confused. She had lost me several yanks back.

Then she did a strange thing. At the head of the bed, she pulled the sheet down over the blanket to form a cuff and then took out of her pocket a six-inch ruler.

"I'm going to measure the distance," she said, "from the top edge of the top sheet to the top edge of the blanket. It must measure six inches, and the cuff must also measure exactly six inches. The portion of undersheet that's exposed and the cuff over the blanket must be exactly the same — not six and one-eighth inches, not five and seven-eighths inches, but exactly six inches in both places." Oh, boy.

The rest was a repetition of what had gone before — the corners at the foot, the sides tucked in tightly so the bed looked like a breadboard with a six-inch cuff. With the pillow in place, the bed was finished. I must admit, I had never seen a bed quite like it.

"That's it," she said. "Now, before you make your own beds, we'll have one more demonstration, this time by one of you."

I don't know what there is about me. Let my name be one of two to be pulled out of a hat to win a trip to Hawaii, I'm not picked. Let me buy a raffle ticket in a sale that features 250 prizes, with 251 tickets sold — you guessed it, I'm not picked. But let me drive on a highway at five miles an hour over the speed limit with cars whizzing past me at twenty miles an hour faster still, that's when I'm picked. I'm the one the trooper nabs. So why should this day be any different?

Maybe things would have been otherwise had I found a taller woman to hide behind. But there were only five-feet-threes, -fours, and -fives in my immediate vicinity, no adequate shields for a five-foot-six, so no amount of crouching helped. The finger of doom found me. "You," its owner said. "Would you like to try?"

I had a choice?

Everybody gathered around my bed. As you can well imagine, I was terribly nervous, and as I ripped the sheets and blankets off with my ten thumbs, my hands were shaking. With twenty-five pairs of critical eyes observing my every shivering movement, I expected to remember nothing, so when I did recall that the sheets came before the blanket, I was considerably encouraged. Then I got to my first corner, I lifted, I tucked, I pulled, and I pushed, and my corner came out round and sloppy. So I yanked, and I smoothed, and I jabbed and I hooked, and my corner came out round and sloppy.

Lieutenant Bolton said, "You have to get it tight — real, real tight," which was exactly what I felt like getting.

My bed got done, of course, although not exactly in record time, and not without a few generous assists from the good Lieutenant. You can imagine my relief when this ordeal was over. My cup of happiness overflowed when Lieutenant Bolton announced she was going to the squadroom below and then would be back to tell us about inspection, and that in the meantime, each woman was to make her bed but that mine could stay. Gladly would I have slept on the floor for the remainder of basic training rather than disturb one hair of its majestic perfection.

Then a horrible thought crossed my mind. Suppose some jealous wiseguy sorehead decided to punch a hole in the middle of my breadboard, or turned my cuff down to six-and-a-half inches, or committed some other reprehensible act of vandalism? The thought was too dreadful to contemplate. I rushed over to my wall closet and grabbed my tennis racket (equipment, athletic). I leaped up on my footlocker, brandished the racket over my head menacingly, and threatened:

"Who touches a hair of yon brown bed
Gets a hit from me right on the head!"

I did it, and I'm glad. It was the only time I got to use my tennis racket while I was in the service.

Nobody was paying any attention to me. All over the room, women were frantically piling up blankets and sheets on their footlockers, and the pulling and the yanking was starting. I saw Trudy struggling to achieve a taut bottom sheet.

"I'll help you," I offered. "You pull and I'll yank."

We did fine together, until we got to the six inches of exposed bottom sheet and the six-inch cuff. Without a ruler, how did one measure exactly six inches?

"I wish I had known," I said to Trudy. "I could have made a fortune selling six-inch rulers to the WAACs. Maybe it's not too late. I could write to Milton Bradley."

"Great," said Trudy. "You do that. But what do I do for now?"

"We'll figure something out," I assured her.

I was standing in the aisle between Trudy's bed and mine. I had an idea. I turned to face my bed, and then, with my two forefingers, I measured the six-inch cuff. I turned slowly — very slowly — careful not to disturb the six-inch distance between fingers. With my elbows resting on my hips and my forefingers extended like Two-Gun Annie, I bent toward Trudy's bed. Quickly, she yanked a little here and pulled a little there, and we had licked the problem.

Apparently this little scene had been witnessed by a number of women, for they began to converge on my bed like locusts on a grain field. Then, with forefingers in front of them exactly six inches apart, slowly and carefully they dispersed in all directions to their respective beds with cries of "Don't come near me," and "Out of my way!" Suddenly someone who was standing next to my bed shrieked, "Guess what! I just measured the cuff with the toothbrush, and the GI toothbrush is exactly six inches long."

The fingers dropped as women scrambled for their toothbrushes. Sure enough, all GI toothbrushes *were* exactly six inches long. There went my fortune.

With the beds made and the footlockers arranged according to the model, everything was lined up — the beds, the six-inch cuffs, the footlockers. For the first time since our arrival the night before, the room was neat, orderly, and military looking. When Lieutenant Bolton returned, she said, "That's fine. This is what your squadroom should always look like in the future." Hm. Some future — putting things, including myself, into an unswerving line.

Trailing behind the Lieutenant were the twenty-five women from the squadroom below. We sat two to a footlocker while Lieutenant Bolton stood in the aisle at the back of the room and explained the meaning of inspection.

Every WAAC would be responsible for her own area, which included her bed, her wall cupboard, her wall locker, her footlocker, and half the floor area on both sides and in front of her bed. In addition, each WAAC would have an additional duty as listed on a weekly duty roster. These duties included cleaning the outside stairway and its landing; the inside stairway that led to the latrines; the corridor outside the latrines; and the latrines. Cleaning the latrines included the wash bowls and the room in which they were located; the shower stalls and the room in which they were located; and the toilet bowls and the room in which they were located. The duty roster would also list the policing of the outside area around the barracks, which meant picking up papers and, heaven forbid, cigarette butts and matches.

That night, when we went to bed, every last girl prayed: Please, God, not the latrines.

On Monday through Friday, Lieutenant Bolton would make a daily inspection at some time when we were engaged in an activity away from the barracks. Saturday morning inspection, however, was something else again. That ceremony would be conducted by the Company Commander followed by the three Platoon Commanders as we stood at attention next to our open footlockers. Four pairs of hypercritical eyes (five, counting Lieutenant Sommers') would sweep the barracks, ghoulishly eager to pounce on an infraction such as a spot on the uniform; a hair on the collar; one shoe protruding one-eighth of an inch beyond the edge of the bed in the line of footwear under it; a shoe not polished to a spittin' shine; a shoelace not tied neatly; bedroom slippers to the right of the shoes instead of to the left; the buckle of a galosh unbuckled; a spot of dust anywhere; a spot of floor unscrubbed anywhere; a six-and-one-eighth-inch cuff on the blanket or exposed undersheet; red nail polish; too much lipstick; a five-and-seven-eighth-inch cuff on the blanket or exposed undersheet.

And what would be the reward for a spotless, gleaming, decontaminated, pasteurized, shipshape barracks and person? Nothing.

What would be the penalty for a bed one-quarter inch out of line? A demerit commonly known as a gig. Gigs would be posted daily, and too great an accumulation of them would result in company punishment, which could be (1) a mere reprimand; (2) a restriction to barracks during off hours; (3) extra fatigue duties (work); or (4) a combination of any of the foregoing.

"Any questions?" asked Lieutenant Bolton. Was she kidding? Who could talk?

It was 4:30, and the next half-hour was a rest period. When the whistle blew at five o'clock, the company formed in front of the barracks for retreat. We stood in parade rest position — feet apart and hands clasped behind our backs — and we could hear, but couldn't see, a trumpeter play "To the Color," and we knew, but couldn't see, that a flag somewhere was being lowered. It was the ceremony that marked the end of the working day.

From retreat, we went to supper. By now, totally oblivious to the noise, I comfortably ate the fried pork chops, applesauce, baked sweet potato, mixed green salad, celery, pickles, bread and butter, cookies, and coffee. (In 1945, the army published a report stating that it had saved $2.7 million on the diet of its female soldiers because they did not want fried potatoes for breakfast, one egg was enough, and they ate less pastry than the men).

After supper, Trudy and I took a short walk, and

then we returned to the barracks. I was weary, not so much from the activities of the day as from the nerve-splintering demands of the damned whistle and the equilibrium-shattering suddenness of officer appearances. We chatted and relaxed, I wrote a few letters, and thus ended my first day as a WAAC recruit at Fort Des Moines. I was on my way toward becoming a soldier — brave, tried, and true khaki.

CHAPTER TEN

Hut-Two-Three-Clickety-Cha

The next morning, I hurried from the mess hall. With only half an hour remaining before our first formation at eight o'clock, I was apprehensive. How could I do all my chores in the short space of half an hour and emerge gigless from the first barracks inspection? Given my extreme maladroitness, it seemed impossible, and my concern was considerably heightened by an observation I had made before leaving the barracks for breakfast. Many of the beds looked as if they had hardly been slept in. Mine resembled the aftermath of a typhoon.

I'm a restless sleeper. From the moment my body hits the mattress, I toss and I flip over, I flail my arms and I flip over, I flail my legs and I flip over, I surround my pillow and I flip over. I crawl to the foot of the bed, I crawl to the middle of the bed, I crawl to the side of the bed, I hang my head over. Then I flip again. As a result of my nocturnal peregrinations, my bottom sheet is under the mattress, my blankets are on the floor, my pillow is hung up on the spring, and I'm lucky if I'm not hung up on the bedpost.

Obviously, the stationary sleepers had the advantage. Some quick tugs here and there, a few well-placed pats, a fast puff of the pillow, and all evidence of occupancy was removed. Not so with me. I had to start, not from scratch, but from behind it.

I hastened up the steps and to my bed. Quickly, I unrolled my bottom sheet. I retrieved the top sheet, the blanket, and the pillow from their sundry landing places, and then, with the utmost care, I repeated each step of the bed-making procedure. Happily, I reaped the benefits of my nervous performance of the day before, for, although I never would have dreamed it myself, my corners were perfect. Not the rest of the bed — only the corners. The bed had a distinct sag in the middle.

I checked my watch. It was a quarter of eight. I still had to line up my footwear, sweep my portion of the floor, and, as shown by the newly posted duty roster for the week, do my extra duty — the latrines, so what else is new?

I tugged the blanket in the lower left corner and tucked it under the mattress, then flew to the lower right and repeated, then to upper right and upper left much like an actor in an old-time movie. Next, I grabbed the broom from Trudy, who had to finish sweeping with her clothes brush, and feverishly swept my half of all sides of my bed; then I rushed down to join the other latrine maids and gave a swish, a swosh and a couple of flushes. I had just lined up my shoes when the "fall out" whistle blew. I was breathless but ready.

Today we were placed into military platoon formation. There would be no more higgledy-piggledy convergence to the front of the barracks. Each platoon was lined up single file, tallest to shortest, and then put into five squads, each squad consisting of ten women abreast of one another. This would be the formation for roll call, for announcements, for ceremonies, and for instruction in many of the military practices. (With specific places assigned, forming the platoon was much more orderly. The first few times there were some collisions, but after a day or two, we ducked and dodged gracefully and arrived in our designated places in a matter of seconds.)

This was the day for learning military practices. Before the flag was lowered at five o'clock, we would know how to stand at attention, how to face, how to march, and how to salute.

Most of us had little trouble achieving the proper "attention" position: heels together, head up, chin in, shoulders back, stomach in, weight slightly forward, arms hanging straight but loosely close to the body — a straight line from head to toe veering slightly from the perpendicular and with unmoving eyes staring straight ahead. As Lieutenant Sommers gave the instructions, the WAAC Platoon Officers walked among us tapping a shoulder here and poking a stomach there. In some cases, the correction helped; in some cases it didn't. The Lieutenant, standing in front of a woman, might say, "Pull in the chin," and out would pop the stomach; or she might correct another woman with "Pull in that rear," and the elbows would fly up and out. These women came into the army looking like a series of S-curves in a tortuous road, and they went out looking the same way.

Facing came next — to the right, to the left, right oblique (pronounced o-blike), left oblique (pronounced the same), and about. Now, we've all seen soldiers in the movies facing right when they should be facing left, and facing left when they should be facing right. These were scenes invented by comedy writers for laughs — right? Wrong. They weren't invented, they happened. I saw them myself. At the command, "Right face!" I'd make a quarter-turn to the right, expecting to see the back of the head of my neighbor, but instead I'd come face to face with her.

"About face" brought even bigger surprises. Correctly executed, it involves placing the right toe behind the left heel. A swivel to the right on the right toe and the left heel brings the swiveler in a position facing in the opposite direction with heels together and toes apart. Many of the women had trouble with this one, and the result was a variety of arriving positions. The most popular had the right foot in front of the left foot (from swiveling either on both toes or on both heels). Next in popularity was arrival only a quarter of the way around (from not swiveling far enough). But my neighbor on the left was the best. She arrived facing in the opposite direction with her feet together, except that her ankles were crossed (from being pretty dumb). When she began to teeter like a circus tightrope walker, I grabbed her and held her even though I knew by this time that it was against the rules. In any kind of military formation, if your nose runs you let it run, if your stocking falls you let it fall, and if your neighbor drops you let her drop. But this lady weighed 180 pounds, and they were all dropping in my direction. I was in no mood for becoming flat as a pancake, especially since nature had already done a pretty good job of it without the lady's help.

Marching came next. It was my favorite. There has always been something about the rhythmical beat of marching and its symmetrical togetherness that stirs me to the fingertips. Even today, when I hear a military band my head flies up, my shoulders spring back, and I walk proudly to the rhythm of the martial music. If the martial music happens to be coming from the television set, I leap up and mark time in front of my chair until my downstairs neighbor bangs the ceiling with her broom.

Each platoon was led to a separate clearing a short distance away from the barracks. Here we received our first instructions in marching from our respective Platoon Commanders. It was really quite simple. All it required was a knowledge of the numbers from one to four and the ability to lift the feet two inches from the ground and keep them moving at 120 steps a minute.

Somehow, everybody seemed to like marching and had little trouble with it — everybody, that is, except Brenner. Brenner didn't like to march. Besides looking like a half-eaten pretzel full of S-curves, Brenner didn't know how to march. She knew how to count to four (I think), but she couldn't bring her foot down on the count. When the Lieutenant chanted,

"HUT-TWO-THREE-FOUR," and we marched forward proudly, our arms swinging at our sides, our feet kept time to the count. But not Brenner's feet. When we were on the left foot, she was on the right foot; when we were going up she was coming down; and always, but always, she was a hut behind. So, instead of the sharp cadence of marching feet, ONE-TWO-THREE-FOUR, we had a staccato-like syncopated rhythm: one-a, two-a, three-a, four-a, clickety, clackety, clickety, clackety, one-a, two-a, three-a, four-a, clickety, clackety, clickety, clackety . . .

The Lieutenant called, "PLATOON, HALT! ONE, TWO!". . . three. That was Brenner.

Lieutenant Bolton approached her. "You're Brenner, aren't you?"

"Yes, ma'am."

"Please try to keep in step, Brenner."

"Yes, ma'am."

"If you find yourself on the wrong foot while marching, put one foot behind the other and do a little hop between counts, like this," and she demonstrated.

"You see, Brenner?"

"Yes, ma'am."

Maybe she did. Except the changeover from one foot to the other didn't seem to get to the root of the problem at all, because here's what happened next.

"PLATOON, MARK TIME, MARCH! FORWARD MARCH! HUT, TWO, THREE, FOUR," clickety, clackety, clickety, clackety. "BREN-NER, GET-IN-STEP", cha, cha, cha-cha-cha. "HUT, TWO," clickety, clackety, "BREN-NER, GET-IN-STEP," cha, cha, cha-cha-cha.

Poor Brenner. She was trying to get on the correct foot and she wound up dancing. And this poor little pretzel danced no better than she marched. Her gangling body flopped along the road as if all her joints were loose.

Everybody felt extremely sorry for poor Brenner. In the half hour we had left before mess, we tried to help her in the barracks.

"On the count of one," we said, "put your left foot down. Good. On the count of two, put your right foot down. Great. Now the left. Now the right. Left, right. Left, right. Left, right, left, right, hut, two, three four," clickety clackety, clickety, clackety, cha, cha, cha-cha-cha.

"Try counting by yourself," someone suggested. "Move your feet together with your lips." Personally, I didn't have much faith that she could do two things at the same time, but she did try.

"One-two-three-four, one-two-three-four," counted Brenner. It was no good. Her lips were in cadence but not her feet. She clacked when she should have clicked, clicked when she should have clacked, and cha'd when I, in a similar position, would have screamed, "BUG OFF!"

We were all positive poor Brenner was going to have a bad time of it in the army. Shortly after basic training was over, I learned that poor Brenner had clicked her way right to Officer Candidate School (where she graduated third from the bottom of her class), and that shortly thereafter, she had clacked herself right into First Lieutenant.

After chow, we learned how to salute. I wish this form of greeting could be extended to all persons in military uniform instead of being limited to the greeting between officer and officer, and to enlisted person to officer in recognition of superior rank. I think this military greeting is one of the friendliest customs of the service. By virtue of their unique garb, strangers who meet on the street are drawn together in brief recognition of their common roles in the affairs of their fellow persons. For a fleeting moment, stripes, bars, maple leaves, and eagles merge into an identity that makes all their wearers brothers and sisters under the insignia.

The history of the salute goes back a long way. In the age of chivalry, when two mounted knights met, it was the custom for each to raise his visor with his right hand while holding the reins of his horse with his left. The gesture was a sign of friendship and confidence because, in addition to exposing the features, it also — which was more important — removed the hand from the vicinity of the weapon. This type of greeting carried over into later periods when European soldiers carrying arms met and raised their right hands to show that they held no weapons and that the meeting was a friendly one. Even in civilian life, when gentlemen went about clothed in heavy capes under which they carried swords, they threw their capes back when meeting a friend, disclosing that the right hand was not on the sword hilt.

Thus, from the practices of our suspicious forbears have come some of our present-day customs (the next time a friend raises his hand in greeting or puts it out for you to shake, you'll know the message is really "See, I'm not going to kill you"), and the knightly gesture of raising the hand to the visor has come to be recognized as the proper greeting between soldiers.

At first, we saluted by the numbers. "One" meant bring the right hand up to the right eye slightly right of center (or to that position on the visor if the hat was being worn), with the fingertips down to the elbow making a perfect line like the hypotenuse of a triangle. "Two" meant drop the hand smartly to the side. This version wasn't as sporty as the unauthorized salute the officers were using — a quick flip of the hand outward from the eye — but it was a distinct improvement over our untutored efforts of the past day and a half when we didn't know any rules and had been saluting when and how we thought we should.

Our ignorance produced some beauts. I saw women saluting with the palm of the hand facing outward, British style; by placing the right hand horizontally over the right eye, palm facing downward, in the style of Columbus looking for America; by placing the right hand so close to the nose that a tiny move of the thumb could have spelled trouble — real, real trouble; with the fingers dangling downward over the eye and the wrist pointing toward the sky, forming a kind of question mark. Then there were the two WAACs walking together who met two officers. One WAAC saluted twice in rapid succession, and the other saluted with both hands. That wasn't right, we learned, and we also learned it isn't necessary to salute when leading a horse, playing baseball, or wheeling a baby carriage, all of which relieved me no end.

The last activity of this second afternoon was physical training, for which we changed into our fatigue clothes — the short, striped seersucker button-down front, belted jobs; the soft, khaki, Jeep-type hats; the khaki anklets; and the sneakers.

On the way out to the front of the barracks, we passed the bulletin board, and lo! there it was — the first gig sheet — the result of our first barracks inspection. At the risk of being late for formation, we crowded excitedly round it, each of us praying silently. Number four read: Blumenthal . . . bobby pin on blanket.

I placed my hands on my hips and jumped to stride position. I touched my right toe with my left hand. I touched my left toe with my right hand. I lay with my face in the dirt and I pushed up. But my heart wasn't in it. During my breakneck last-minute preparations that morning, a bobby pin must have fallen from my upswept coiffure. Damn those bobby pins! They were the same khaki color as the blanket.

CHAPTER ELEVEN

A Ditch In Time

Before the week was out, I had become unerringly disciplined to the demands of the clock; it hadn't taken me long to recognize I had damned well better do so, or I would soon become disciplined to the demands of a summary court-martial. Our activities adhered closely to the same daily schedule, so, although I might postpone necessary duties until the last possible moment, procrastinator that I am, I did manage to scuttle to the right place at the right time.

The Monday through Friday schedule was as follows:

5:45	Reveille — awake to the boom of a cannon
6:00	A whistle blows for "lights on" in the barracks, which means get the hell out of bed
6:43	A whistle blasts shrilly
6:43:01	A voice booms, "Fall out!"
6:43:02	I fall out
6:45	Company forms in front of the barracks for roll call and announcements
7:00	We march to mess
7:30	We prepare barracks for inspection
8:00	Classes are conducted in the barracks

11:00	Whistle blows to fall out for close-order drill
11:00:01	I fall out
11:00:02	Close order drill
11:30	Rest
12:00	We march to chow
1:00	Classes in the barracks
4:00	Whistle blows to fall out for physical training
4:00:01	I fall out
4:00:02	Physical training
4:30	Rest
5:00	Whistle blows to fall out for retreat
5:00:01	I fall out
5:00:02	Retreat — end-of-day ceremony during which the company stands in front of the barracks at "Parade Rest" position while a trumpeter somewhere plays "To the Color," and somewhere a flag is lowered
5:10	More chow
5:40	Off duty
9:00	Tattoo. No, no. This only means "Lights out" in the squadroom. (If I want to continue to write letters or to read, it is Onward, Jewish Soldier, to the latrine).
11:00	Bed check — a Lieutenant flashes a searchlight in your face just as you drop off to sleep

The classes in the barracks conducted twice a day were lectures by the Platoon Commanders. Each of the three platoons gathered in one of its two squadrooms; the women sat two to a footlocker for the purpose of being indoctrinated with certain:

a. Sections of the Articles of War: required to be read to every enlisted person every six months — date of reading to be recorded in each person's 201 file.

b. Army Regulations: For instance, paragraph 2e of AR 600-1 stated that no military person was permitted to give a gift to a superior in the service — a regulation totally superfluous for us, since we couldn't even afford the postage stamp to send home for postage stamps.

c. Military Customs and Courtesies: Never volunteer excuses or explain a shortcoming unless you are sure an explanation is required. (I was sure; a lot of good it did me.)

d. Rules About Wearing the Uniform: Uniforms must be neat and clean and must be buttoned at all times.

(It was obvious that c and d meant "Always keep your uniform and your lip buttoned.")

On Thursday of that first week, at the noon formation, we were surprised to see, standing next to Lieutenant Sherman, a male Lieutenant who was not Lieutenant Sommers. He was introduced to us as Lieutenant Bentley, our new Company Commander.

Back in the barracks after chow, Trudy and I speculated.

"What do you suppose happened to Lieutenant Sommers?" I asked. "Do you think he was fired?"

"Out of the army?"

"Well, I can hope, can't I? He must have been

transferred. But why?"

"For no reason, probably," answered Trudy.

"There has to be a reason," I insisted.

"Not in the army, there doesn't," corrected Trudy.

"Well, whatever happened or for whatever reason, I'm glad."

"Why? You've had no trouble in the last couple of days."

"I know. But I was forever expecting it. I'm quite relieved. As a matter of fact, I think I'll go down to the PX and celebrate."

"Celebrate! At the PX? With what? A double scoop of ice cream?

"Yep — one pineapple and one chocolate."

"Aren't you the reckless one with your twenty-one dollars a month? I suppose when we get our raise to fifty dollars, you'll get a third scoop."

"Strawberry. I also want to buy cigarettes and some bobby pins that aren't khaki. Maybe they come in pink."

I walked leisurely, enjoying the unseasonably warm, balmy September evening. It took me about ten minutes to reach the PX. I had made my purchases and was getting my change when a voice behind me said, "Good evening."

I turned to see who was addressing me. To my utter astonishment, I came face to face with the ubiquitous Lieutenant Sommers. My first reaction was that there must have been a "disaster area" sign around somewhere I had missed.

"Oh. Good evening, sir," I said respectfully.

"What a nice surprise," said the Lieutenant.

What on earth was he talking about? Was this the calm before the chopping block? What was I doing wrong? Was it after bed check? Was my uniform unbuttoned? Was my slip showing? Was I off limits?

I explained quickly, "I was just buying some cigarettes, sir."

"I see," he said. "Did you know I'm no longer with your company?"

"Yes, sir. The new Company Commander was introduced to us. I was sorry to hear you had left, sir." May God forgive me.

"I'm now Executive, Supply, and Mess Officer with a male company."

"I hope you like your new assignment. Now, I have to go, sir."

"Don't rush off. You look pretty nifty in that uniform. You're what a WAAC should look like."

"Thank you, sir. I must go."

"But then, you looked pretty nifty in Philadelphia, too."

"You recognized me?" I shrieked. In shock, I forgot to "sir."

"Of course."

"When?"

"I saw your name on the company roster before I saw you."

"You remembered my name . . . sir? Of course, how could you forget?"

His eyes twinkled. "I remembered the names of all the women who made swan dives onto my desk."

I felt myself blush. He must have noticed, for he smiled and said reassuringly, "As I recall, you gave a pretty good account of yourself."

"The answer I gave you about the Nazis wasn't very good."

"Well, we all get pretty emotional about the Nazis. I might have answered the same way under the strain of an interview."

I doubted it, but he *was* being kind.

"So when I fell out late that first day, you knew who I was."

"Of course. Was I very unkind?"

"Very, sir."

"I'm sorry."

I couldn't believe what was happening. This was Lieutenant Sommers, and he sounded almost human and was talking to me as if I was somebody. I decided I had better get on my way before I found myself not hating him.

"I have to go now, sir. Good night, sir."

"Where are you going?"

"Back to the barracks."

"May I walk you back?"

"Oh, no, sir. I'll be all right, sir."

"But I'd like to."

This entire episode was like some incredible dream. We walked down the stairs together, and when we reached the bottom, he said, "Instead of going right back, how about a walk?"

"Oh, I couldn't, sir."

"Why not?"

"Well, uh — I have to be back before bed check, sir."

"But that's not until eleven. It's only eight-thirty."

"I'm sorry, sir, it's against army regulations, sir."

"To walk?"

"No, sir. I don't want to get into trouble, sir. You're an officer and I'm an enlisted woman, and we're not supposed to fraternize, sir."

He grinned. "Tell you what. We won't fraternize. We'll just walk," and he touched my elbow lightly and steered me in the direction away from the WAAC area and into historical Fort Des Moines.

The picture that most frequently comes to mind at the mention of "army post" is the traditional row after row of white, wooden, double-storied barracks as far as the eye can see, with here and there some single-storied structures that house administrative offices, commissaries, warehouses and mess halls. Usually, completing the picture, recalcitrant soldiers sit outside peeling potatoes. (Fort Des Moines must have had its share of recalcitrant soldiers, but either they were assigned to a different punitive chore or they peeled inside, for I never saw an outside potato peeler.)

Fort Des Moines had a more permanent look. It had been established as a cavalry post for career soldiers in 1901, when horsemen still played an important part in the military. After the introduction of mechanized and armored warfare, it was used as a training camp for Negro officers during World War I and, after that war, became a hospital for the rehabilitation of soldiers returned from overseas, until the Women's

Army Auxiliary Corps was activated and it was selected as the headquarters and first WAAC training center.

As we passed the various buildings, Lieutenant
Sommers explained their functions. He had preceded
me to the fort by several weeks and, apparently out of
curiosity, had done some research.

Along one side of the elm-shaded parade ground
were red-brick L-shaped structures that looked more
like big Colonial houses than army barracks. They had
pointed slate roofs, iron-railed porches front and back,
ceiling-to-floor round columns, and neatly trimmed
shrubbery.

"These used to be the barracks for enlisted men,"
explained Lieutenant Sommers, "so they lent themselves quite easily to billeting WAAC officer trainees.
They just had to make some small changes."

"Like what?" I asked innocently.

"Like adapting the latrines for female use."

"Oh."

Facing the other three sides of the parade ground
were more barracks as well as other buildings of
similar design: the Bachelor Officers' Quarters (BOQ),
where an unmarried commissioned officer enjoyed
the luxury of a room to himself; units for married
commissioned and noncommissioned officers and
their families; consolidated mess halls that could feed
several companies of soldiers at one time; the Post
Guard House, identified by the small shingle hanging over the top of the stairway; and, of course, the
most popular building on the post, the Post Exchange, or PX.

As we passed a row of buildings almost at the entrance to the fort, Lieutenant Sommers said, "Some day, when you're down this way, go inside one of these buildings. You'll enjoy it."

"What are they, sir?"

"These are the former stables. They still have their high, vaulted ceilings with wagon wheels suspended from their beams. Even though the horses and the horsemen have long since disappeared into limbo, there's no mistaking that these were once stables."

"How interesting. I must make a point of visiting here."

"I think you'll get a real feeling of history."

"What are they used for now, sir?"

"They were converted into barracks some time ago. The plans are to use them as a staging area for the WAACs."

"What's that?"

"A staging area? It's a place where troops are assembled and readied for transfer to other places."

"I suppose some of the first WAAC arrivals will be ready to go out soon."

"In a week or two, I imagine. But the WAACs have used the stables already. When Colonel Faith, the Commandant of Fort Des Moines, first learned of the imminent arrival of the first WAAC officer candidates, the barracks intended for their use were still in the process of alteration. He had to find other billeting quarters in a hurry, and the only barracks available were the stables. That's where the first WAAC officer candidates were sent."

"Oh ho. That explains a few things."

"What things?"

"The charming soubriquets — why some of the WAAC oppositionists were referring to the WAACs as — excuse the expression, sir — WAAC-asses."

He laughed. "Incidentally, since I'm excusing your expression, now would you do me a favor?"

"What's that, sir?"

"Cut out a few 'sirs'!"

He noticed the puzzled look on my face. "What's the matter?" he asked.

"You're so different."

"From Philadelphia?"

"And from my first fall-out."

He looked amused. "I had to project the army image, you know."

"If you don't mind my saying so, sir . . ."

"Uh-uh-uh."

"If you don't mind my saying so, don't you think you overprojected a wee bit?"

"Maybe. But then, how else could I have shown how important I was?"

"Now you're joking."

"Well . . . maybe." He thought for a moment and then added, "And maybe not."

It had grown dark, but the lampposts provided good illumination. We circumnavigated the parade ground, and then penetrated the interior with its various warehouses, commissaries, and administrative buildings.

Lieutenant Sommers told me he was a practicing

lawyer in Philadelphia. He had been in the army about six months and thus far had been receiving temporary duty assignments while awaiting orders for a promised assignment to the Judge Advocate General's Department.

We had walked for a long time when, reaching a lamppost, I stopped to glance at my watch.

"Good heavens! It's almost ten-thirty. I have to get back."

"OK. We can go through here. It's a shortcut."

He led me to a narrow path between a row of trees, and we headed in the direction of the WAAC area. Once outside the main post, there were long stretches of almost total darkness. I was about to reach for the small flashlight I carried in my utility bag when, suddenly, a voice boomed out of the darkness, "HALT! WHO GOES THERE?"

Lieutenant Sommers gave me a shove, and I went flying sideways over the ground to land face down in a muddy ditch just as a flashlight shone in the Lieutenant's face.

"It's OK, guard. I'm Lieutenant Sommers."

"ADVANCE AND BE RECOGNIZED! Oh, good evening, sir. Are you alone? I thought I heard voices."

"Yes, I'm alone. Just taking a walk. I was singing."

"Good enough, sir. Good night, sir."

"Good night . . . Oh, guard."

"Yes, sir?"

"Could you walk me over into the lighted area? It's quite dark and I don't have a flashlight with me."

"Certainly, sir."

Lieutenant Sommers led the guard away from my muddy sanctuary, and as soon as I felt it was safe, I climbed out, reached for my flashlight, and scampered as fast as I could in the direction of the barracks. Breathlessly, I approached the vicinity of the orderly room. As I scooted past it, I doused my light, and I could see Lieutenant Mansfield, the WAAC OD (Officer of the Day), just rising from her desk and reaching for her flashlight. She was preparing to come to the barracks for bed check! When I reached the bottom of the barracks stairway, I glanced back and saw the lighted flashlight emerging from the orderly room. Up the stairs I flew as silently as I could and into the squadroom. I tripped over a few footlockers and hissed "Sh-h-h-h" to a few heads I saw rising from their pillows. I reached my bed, kicked off my shoes, threw my hat under my bed, hopped under the covers and pulled them up to my chin. And not a moment too soon. From bed to bed went the light to determine with certainty that each one held a form. When the light reached the form on fourth bed on the left, it was fa-a-st asleep.

As soon as the Lieutenant was gone, I reached for my pajamas and ripped off my clothes, dropping them on the floor. The following morning, getting rid of the dried mud was a pain, but with double-quick movements and Trudy's help, my bed, my clothes, and I were shining and ready for the whistle.

That evening after supper, the squadroom was full of action. We were going full steam ahead with our preparations for our first Saturday inspection when a

WAAC appeared in the doorway and called, "Anyone by the name of Blumenthal here?"

"Yes," I answered, looking up from my scrub position on the floor. "Right here. What is it?"

"There's a phone call for you in the dayroom."

I dropped my scrub brush, rose from my knees, and ran down the stairs. It could only be a call from home. Maybe my last letter hadn't arrived.

"Hello," I said into the wall telephone.

"Hi. This is Peter."

"Who?"

"Peter. Peter Sommers."

"Oh. Hi."

"I'm sorry about what happened last night."

"Oh, no harm done," I assured him, as though falling headfirst into the mud was something I did every day just for kicks.

"When that guard called 'Halt,' a crazy thing happened. The first thing that came to my mind was what you had said about regulations and fraternizing and your getting into trouble. Immediately, I realized what a silly thing I had done, but it was too late. Did I hurt you? Did I push you very hard?"

"No, you didn't hurt me, and you didn't push me very hard — just enough for me to land in a muddy ditch face down."

"Oh, gosh! I'm sorry. Was it very bad?"

"Well, it wasn't exactly a pink tea."

"I can assure you nothing like that will ever happen again."

You are so right, Lieutenant Sommers, SIR, for you

will never have the opportunity again, SIR. I have had it with you, old boy, SIR.

Aloud I said, "Uh-huh."

"I'll call you," he said. "Goodbye."

CHAPTER TWELVE

Soapsuds Keep Falling From My Skin

Every last WAAC in the squadroom was up and out of bed before reveille the next morning. We were too nervous to wait for the lights, and we had become so proficient at making our beds, we were able to do so by flashlight. By the time the lights went on, the room looked magnificent — GI magnificent, that is. Floors had been scrubbed, wall lockers had been scrubbed, all items in footlockers, wall lockers, and under the beds were in their respective GI places, and everything that could be lined up was lined up, including two flies on the ceiling. By the time we went to breakfast, the barracks were shining, spotless, and ready for inspection. At eight o'clock *we* were shining, spotless, and ready for inspection, standing to the right of our open footlockers in position to snap to attention at the call.

"Attention!" called the WAAC nearest the door as the first visored head appeared in the doorway.

We snapped to attention. Nobody moved a muscle or an eyeball.

Five people entered the room in a line (how else?). Leading the parade was Lieutenant Bentley, our new male Company Commander, followed by Lieutenant Sherman, our acting WAAC Company Commander, who was followed by our Lieutenant Bolton, who was followed by Lieutenants Mansfield and Simon. Lieutenant Bolton carried a pad and a pencil. As each officer passed a unit consisting of one bed, one wall locker, one footlocker, one row of footwear under the bed, one floor area six feet wide and eight feet long, and one upright, rigid body, the officer's eyes swept over the bed, the wall locker, the footlocker, the footwear, the floor, and rigid body, one of which had stopped breathing. Up one side they went and down the other — five sober, grim-visaged, ultracritical, hairsplitting fussbudgets in search of a mistake.

Because circumstances prevented our looking to the right or to the left, the only way we could determine when the last officer had disappeared out the door would be when she called "At ease!" just before stepping out. However, this last officer forgot. We knew they were gone when the WAAC nearest the door threw herself flat on her back on the floor, threw her hat up in the air, and yelled "Whoopee!" Whereupon we all collapsed — some on the floor, some on footlockers, and some — yes — on their beds, for, from now until Monday morning inspection, our squadroom could be a pigsty, if we so chose, and some of us so chose.

We were jubilant because the first Saturday inspection was behind us and because it had been a gigless inspection for our squadroom. Lieutenant Bolton hadn't written one thing on her pad. For me, it was a very special occasion: my first gigless inspection. Every day that week I had been on the gig list, as follows:

Tues.	Blumenthal . . .	bobby pin on bed
		(that was the first day)
Weds.	Blumenthal . . .	wrinkle in blanket
		(one tug too few)
Thurs.	Blumenthal . . .	cuff 6 ⅛ inches
		(I relied on my eye to
		measure)
Fri.	Blumenthal . . .	Toothbrush on bed
		(I didn't rely on my
		eye to measure)

It was a close call. I had made up my mind that if I received a gig on Saturday, the next gig sheet would read:

Mon.	Blumenthal . . .	lifeless body on bed
		(No more gigs)

By the hundreds, happily and eagerly, like prisoners in a jailbreak, the WAACs poured out of Fort Des Moines that Saturday after the noon mess. Outside the fort, buses waited to transport us to the city of Des Moines. Just as the last WAAC on a bus had pulled in her butt and the driver had forced the door closed behind her and pulled out, another bus would pull up. They left every three minutes, and we were queued up for half a mile.

The city of Des Moines swarmed with WAACs, or, as some Des Moines citizens put it, was "infested" with them. Probably fifteen hundred of us contributed to making Des Moines a city of khaki that day. We strolled through the streets in twos and threes and took pictures on the steps of the State Capitol. We drifted in and out of stores, and although we made a few small purchases, mostly the shopping was of the window variety. The highlight of the day was stopping for a soda — pineapple with chocolate ice cream for me. Some of the WAACs who chose to wear civilian clothes (which were permitted off duty while we were not yet part of the army) stopped for some of the stronger stuff.

Most of us returned to the fort for evening mess; nowhere else could we get a meal that cheap. I noticed that Mary Sue, the GI dollie from across the aisle, hadn't come in yet by the time I went to bed, nor was she there all the next day. I hoped she hadn't gone AWOL. But she turned up for reveille on Monday morning and told us she had rented a hotel room in Des Moines, wallowing in the privacy it afforded and emerging only to catch a taxi back to the fort in time for reveille.

On Sunday, the first KP and CQ roster was posted for the coming week. During our four weeks of basic training, each day six WAACs would be assigned for KP (Kitchen Police), and one (the lucky one) each day for CQ (Charge of Quarters) duty. The CQ would spend a full day in the orderly room making herself available to the company officers for errands, answering the telephone, and other clerical duties. She also covered the orderly room after duty hours and slept there on a cot. She would be relieved at eight o'clock when the new

CQ came on duty. The hardest part of the CQ's job was her responsibility for waking the KP, who had to rise at an unearthly hour — which made the CQ's rising hour even more unearthly. Because overall CQ was preferable to KP, it was only natural that on the very first roster, and for the very first day, my name should be listed for you-know-what.

Usually, after "lights out," I, along with other night owls, went down to the latrine to write letters, to read, or just to socialize. But not Sunday. That night I went to bed at "lights out." If I thought retiring at an early hour on Sunday night would prepare me for rising on Monday morning before the dawn had given the slightest thought to cracking, was I ever wrong!

"Go 'way!" I groaned, wrenching my shoulder free from the overly energetic grasp of the conscientious Charge of Quarters.

"Sh-h-h," she whispered. "Come on. The dirty pots await you."

Now, if that isn't adding insult to injury, I don't know what is. And if there's anything I can't stand, it's insults, injuries, bad jokes, crowing Charges of Quarters, and the thought of dirty pots at a quarter to five in the morning.

I had no choice, of course, so, unhappily, I groped my way to my footlocker. I have to admit that with every article in its GI place, finding what I needed in the inky blackness was a cinch, even in my foggy condition. I carried my clothing down to the latrine, where I could have put the lights on if I wanted to, but it mattered little one way or the other. My eyes were closed, anyway. To the best of my knowledge, I arrived in the mess hall with everything on my body that was supposed to go on my body — underwear, fatigue dress, fatigue hat, anklets, and sneakers — but I can't guarantee everything was in its proper place.

Altogether, we were twelve heavy-lidded, unhappy KPs — six from my company and six from the company that shared the mess hall with us. We had breakfast at two tables in an atmosphere that could hardly be called scintillating. The only thing that sparkled was the tableware, in accordance with AR 40-225, PAR 14, which made certain washing procedures mandatory. I was fortunate there was no army regulation that made conversation mandatory, because I had all I could do to open and close my mouth for eating.

While our digestive systems were still struggling with the weirdness of ingesting food at this ghostly hour, a WAAC officer entered the mess hall.

"I'm Lieutenant Overton," she announced, "your mess officer. Sit where you are while I brief you on your duties and responsibilities as kitchen police.

"First, I think it's important that you don't regard kitchen police as a menial assignment. It's far from that. A spotless and orderly mess hall contributes to the efficiency of its operation, and an efficiently operated mess contributes to the morale of an organization. An army composed of cheerful and zealous organizations will win the war."

Well, certainly, I wanted to help win the war, and I couldn't wait to get my hands on a mop.

Next, she outlined the chores, which, she explained, were our responsibility to divide among us. She separated them into three parts: before meals, during meals, and after meals.

Before — Each table was to be supplied with pitchers of water, salt, pepper, ketchup, and other necessary items. Trays and dishes were to be stacked and placed near the service counter for easy accessibility. Utensils were to be separated into knives, forks, and spoons, and placed near the trays.

During — KPs were to make themselves available to the enlisted personnel for the refilling of water pitchers, and to officer personnel for the refilling of anything they wanted refilled. Two KPs were to be stationed at the garbage cans to act as garbage-can police. One KP would forestall the disposal of liquids into the solids can, paper into the liquid can, solids into the paper can, and whatever other possibilities existed. The second KP was to report any WAAC who threw out edible food. (We had been warned about taking only as much as we could eat and eating everything we had taken. More than once I left the mess hall with a cold asparagus tip in my pocket).

After — Trays, dishes, and utensils were to be washed, benches wiped clean, tables scrubbed, and the floor swept and mopped.

After breakfast, I wiped benches, I scrubbed tables, and I swept. After lunch, I washed dishes, I washed dishes, and I washed dishes. There was no end to them. Brigadier General Dwight David Eisenhower was promoted to Major-General, and to Lieutenant General, and to four-star, and to five-star, and still

I washed dishes. The soapsuds and my perspiration mingled as they dropped tenderly from every visible inch of weary skin. The only bright spot of the early afternoon was my awareness of Circular #76, War Department 1941. It stated, "Use of towels or cloths for drying dishes is prohibited. All dishes shall be air dried."

About 3:30, I decided that I had earned a cigarette, and, relieved by a sweeper, I stepped out the back door. It was my first smoke in four hours, and I inhaled deeply, savoring every puff. When I could no longer puff without burning my nose, with deep regret I scattered the remains to the winds like the good soldier I was and prepared to return to the mess hall. Just then, a small delivery-type truck approached and screeched to a sudden stop. From the passenger side jumped a male officer. It was Lieutenant Sommers.

"What are you doing here?" he asked.

"I'm on KP."

"We're on our way to the commissary to pick up some supplies, Come on along."

"Oh, no. I couldn't."

"Come on. You look like you've been working hard."

"No, no. I'm afraid."

"Of what? We'll only be gone about fifteen minutes. Nobody will miss you."

"That's not it."

"It's not? Then what *are* you afraid of?"

"A wheel will fall off the truck."

He laughed. "That won't happen, I promise you.

This is the chance of a lifetime. You may never again have the opportunity of seeing thousands of cans of baked beans all in one place."

"I think I'll survive."

He grabbed my hand and pulled me toward the truck. Before I could say "Lieutenant Sommers, don't!" I was sitting between him and the driver, and we were off to see the commissary — the wonderful commissary of Fort Des Moines, Iowa.

It was a beautiful, warm, sunny September day, the kind on which no mortal should ever have to do KP duty. I tried to feel guilty, but, somehow it didn't quite come off. I did do a little wrestling with my conscience, but my conscience arrived at a rationalization that went something like this: What the heck.

Bumping over the bumps with Peter in a delivery truck was not quite the same as flying about the countryside in a bright red convertible with the top down, but it sure did beat washing dishes. I couldn't help recalling the huge army truck in which I had been transported to the post on the night of my arrival, and, with much satisfaction, I recognized that I was coming up in the army. Trucks were getting smaller, and I had advanced to the front seat.

At the commissary, Peter and his driver hauled cases of foodstuffs onto the truck. We drove back to the mess hall and stopped at the back door. Peter jumped out and helped me off.

"See," he said, "here you are, all in one piece. Now, are you sorry you came along?"

"Of course not. I enjoyed it. Thanks."

I ran the few steps to the building and was about to step inside, when, in the doorway, appeared Lieutenant Overton.

She looked surprised. "Are you on KP duty here?" she asked, her eyes taking in the truck and Peter.

"Y-yes, ma'am."

"What are you doing out here?"

"Hi, there, Marge." Peter had rushed over.

"Hello, Peter."

"How are you?"

"Fine, Peter."

"Haven't seen you over at the Officers' Club lately."

"I guess we've missed each other."

"Why don't you drop in tonight? I'll buy you a drink."

As Peter had intended, I took advantage of this diversionary tactic to slip into the mess hall. Because the fatigue clothes of all the KPs were identical, I knew I could count on getting lost among all the other fatigued bodies. I rushed over to one of the washtubs, pushed aside a grateful WAAC, and in two seconds flat was elbow-deep in soapsuds.

"YOU!" a voice said. I didn't need to turn. I knew.

"What's your name?"

"Auxiliary Blumenthal, ma'am."

"What company?"

"Eight, ma'am."

"KP for you for the next three days. I'll notify your commanding officer."

Lieutenant Sommers, sir, I swear I'll kill you.

CHAPTER THIRTEEN

The Army Doesn't Have Aardvarks

In late September, we received our winter uniforms, the olive drabs. The blouse, beltless and nipping our waists where a waist should be nipped, was more flattering to most of the WAACs than the summer jacket. Notwithstanding the fact that the color made some of our complexions look a little drab and on rainy days a little olive, most of us were happy with it.

In Fort Des Moines, wearing the winter uniform was prescribed for the period from October 1 to April 1. But because the weather was still mild, our utility coats served quite adequately, and when we didn't receive the winter overcoat with the rest of the issue, we assumed the omission was intentional.

Nobody anticipated that an unseasonable cold wave would hit the state of Iowa. From the delights of balmy weather, a sudden temperature drop plunged us into near-freezing cold. The day we had a light snow, we were lucky to have our galoshes. The ground froze, and I was reminded of a little rhyme attributed to Philander Johnson:

Oh, what a blamed uncertain thing
This pesky weather is.
It blew and snew and then it thew,
And now, by jing, it's friz.

We stood in formation, shivering in our Arctic four-buckle galoshes, the multiple sweaters we wore under our utility coats, and our newly issued woolen hose, gloves, and drawers (khaki and droopy). Any one of us could have been used as a flag in the Retreat ceremony: our noses were red, our cheeks were white, and our lips were blue. The ears? We didn't have any. They had dropped off.

The WAAC Company Commanders were frantic that morning at finding themselves without appropriate top covering for their companies. They sped to their respective orderly rooms and instructed their company clerks to prepare requisitions immediately. "Take the requisition to the warehouse as fast as your legs will carry you," they said. "Tell the warehouse to notify us as soon as possible when they would like us to come down for our overcoats."

The action was swift. The very next day we were marched down to the warehouse, where we were issued overcoats. Except they weren't WAAC overcoats — they were thick, heavy, long brown men's overcoats. There were small men's overcoats for the small women, which were too big; there were large overcoats for the large women, which were too big; there were medium-sized overcoats for the medium-sized women, which were too big. Granted, the emergency called for drastic measures, but 34-26-34 women in

46-42-46 overcoats were drastic measures that were a sight to behold. We were covered from the top of the head to the soles of the shoes to the tips of the fingers and a foot or two beyond. When we stood at attention, our sleeves dangled somewhere in the vicinity of the knees, and we executed snappy salutes with the elbows while the sleeve-ends flapped merrily in the zero-temperature breezes. A critical problem was finding a way to minister to a runny nose. Fortunately, the sleeves had no buttons, but the material *was* a little scratchy.

That night Peter called. "How about meeting me at the PX tonight?" he asked.

I hesitated. "How do I know the roof won't cave in?"

"Everything worked out fine the day we went to the commissary, didn't it? I distracted Marge so you could slip into the mess hall."

"I slipped into the mess hall OK, but you didn't distract Marge quite enough."

"What do you mean?"

"I was given three more days of KP."

"What! I thought I had done such a good job."

"Not good enough."

"Meet me tonight. We'll go out on the town. I'll take you to a movie in Des Moines."

I was about to accept, glutton for punishment that I am, when suddenly I remembered the overcoats. "I can't," I said, and I explained about the overcoats.

"Well, you'll certainly be warm enough. What's the problem?"

"The problem is that these overcoats were meant only to be worn, not seen."

"You'll be in the car."

"To get into the theater, I'll have to get out of the car, won't I? Unless you know of another way."

"OK. Then we can just sit in the PX and talk. I'll buy you an ice cream cone."

"All right, but only for a little while. I have a few chores to do. Oh, and one thing."

"Yes?"

"Promise you won't laugh."

"Scout's honor."

That night at seven, I arrived at the steps of the Post Exchange. Peter was already there. When he saw me, he sat down on the steps, and he laughed and laughed and laughed.

"You said the overcoat was big, but you didn't say monstrous. It really is a funny sight. I'm sorry. You look lovely."

"It isn't necessary to overdo it. Just because you laughed, I'm going to have something more than an ice cream cone."

"There's not much more you can get here."

"Ho, HO! That's what you think. I'm going to have an ice cream soda."

We had started up the steps. "Where's your elbow?" Peter asked. "All I'm getting is empty sleeve."

"I can manage. I'll hold up my coat so I don't trip, if I can find my hands, that is."

Peter steered me to the one table in the Post Exchange provided for the GI customers. "What'll you have?" he asked.

"A pineapple soda with chocolate ice cream."

He walked over to the counter and was back in a second.

"No sodas," he said, "only cones."

"In that case, I'll have a cone with two scoops — one pineapple and one chocolate."

He went over to the counter again and was back in a second.

"No pineapple and no chocolate. Only vanilla."

"I hate vanilla."

"Why don't we go to Des Moines? We could find pineapple and chocolate there."

"I'd die first. I'll take vanilla."

While we were munching on our cones, Peter said, "I had to go down to the warehouse today to pick up some clothing for my men, and I asked the Corporal in charge how come the WAACs didn't have overcoats."

"Did he know why?"

"He said the original requisitions for winter issue included the WAAC overcoat, and he did order them. But someone else checked in the clothing when it arrived, and he just assumed the overcoats were there."

"When did he first discover they weren't?"

"When he went to issue the WAACs their winter clothing, he looked high and low for the overcoats and then realized why he couldn't find them."

"Because there weren't any."

"Right."

"It seems inconceivable," I commented, "that the army should have been caught unprepared like this."

"Maybe the coats are still in the process of manufacture."

"But they've known for months that we do exist and that we would need overcoats for the winter."

"Judging from what I've seen the army do with assignments, the sleeve setter-inners were probably former pipe fitters. Maybe that's what's taking so long."

"What a horrible thought!"

"What is?"

"That I might have to walk around with my arms stuck through two pipes when I get my WAAC overcoat."

Peter laughed.

"So what did the Corporal do when he discovered there were no WAAC overcoats?" I asked.

"He realized how serious this could be if we suddenly had a cold wave, which, of course, is exactly what happened. He rushed over to the officers' mess and found Captain Cunningham, the quartermaster, and told him about it."

"And what did he do?"

"He said to prepare endorsements on the requisition and send it up through channels for endorsements."

"Well, that shouldn't have taken very long."

"How little you know about the army! There are as many channels in the army as there are beans."

"Oh?"

"And then the endorsements had to make their way down."

"Through the same channels?"

"Of course. The army never changes beans or channels in the middle of a war."

"And then what happened?"

"I really don't know any more than that. I can only imagine. The requisition must have finally arrived at the desk of Corporal Algernon Agamemnon Jelly."

"Poor guy."

"You feeling sorry for the poor Corporal who does all the work?"

"No, only for his name. What do you suppose happened after that?"

"Probably Corporal Jelly went through his big, black book in which he records all military items from aardvark to zymometer."

"Who would need an aardvark in the army?"

"I don't know. Don't spoil my story."

Then, suddenly, Peter waxed eloquent. In his most superb oratory, and with graceful gesticulations, he declaimed, "And now the horrifying truth burst upon his consciousness like the sudden splinter of a summer thunderstorm upon the bucolic tranquility of slumbering hamlets and pastoral rivulets!"

"You mean, somebody goofed. Right?"

"Right. There were no WAAC overcoats."

"What did he do?"

"I suppose he didn't know what to do. It wouldn't surprise me if he went into the latrine to slit his throat. Now, let's see. What would happen next? Maybe Corporal Murgatroyd Flycatcher comes into the latrine wearing an overcoat, and Algernon has a brainstorm. 'That's it,' he shouts. 'Men's overcoats for the WAACs.' So he prepares an endorsement for Lieutenant Flypaper's signature."

"Wait a minute. That was the Corporal's name."

"No, he was Flycatcher. The Lieutenant is Flypaper."

"And that's how I came to be wearing this Schiaparelli original."

"Who knows? You have to admit, it was a good story."

"True. And now I have to leave."

"Why? You just got here."

"Look at your watch."

"It's twenty minutes to nine. Where did the time go?"

"Into your story."

"You have until eleven."

"I told you I would stay only for a little while. I'll just have time to get back, gather up my writing materials, and get down to the latrine before 'lights out.' If I don't get some letters written home, I'm going to get some frantic phone calls."

"I'll walk you."

"Thank you, but let's not push my luck. Good night."

And, believe it or not, I did make it back to the barracks without any mishaps — that is, if you don't count tripping over my overcoat and falling up the barracks stairs.

That was Tuesday. On Saturday, we had a parade. Behind the male formation on the parade ground stood fifteen hundred overcoats. There were no faces, no feet, only overcoats. The band struck up "The Caissons Go Rolling Along," and the overcoats marched. "Hut-two-three-four" counted the Lieutenants to the beat of the military music. Left-right-left-right went the overcoats.

That night in the barracks, Trudy and I agreed that one addition could have completed the absurdity of this ludicrous picture. We should have been singing a marching song. So we composed one to the tune of "The Caissons."

Over hill, over dale,
We clean up the dusty trail,
As our overcoats go marching along.
First a left, then a right,
Oh, my golly, what a sight,
As our overcoats go marching along.
Look, ma, aren't we neat!
No hands nor any feet,
No shapely chests nor even any throats!
Look at us, holy Moses,
We've no chins nor any noses.
We're just a bunch of marching overcoats.

Over rocks, over sand,
We tramp o'er the dusty land,
As our overcoats go marching along.
Column lefts, column rights,
We perspire like armored knights,
As our overcoats go marching along.
But we wear them without fussin'

Though they're really wearin' us'n,
And the sweat that flows would flood a field of
    oats.
We're hot from head to metatarsus,
Still it's better 'n frozen arses
When we wear these bouncing, marching
    overcoats.

About a week later we received our WAAC overcoats, and it wasn't without some regrets that we
relinquished the men's coats. Despite the limitations
they imposed, we grew to like the roominess. I suppose this was chiefly because we had discovered that,
given the command "Atten-HUT!", we could make
our overcoats stand at attention while we remained at
ease inside.

CHAPTER FOURTEEN

Please Don't
Salute The
Garbage

The days passed quickly. They were hectic days. We hopped from formation to classes to drill to parades to physical training to mess to more formations to more drill to more parades to more physical training and more mess. To say the pace was brisk would be a vast understatement. My poor, aching feet were constantly in high gear. But after the first shock, I adjusted well, for my legs were long and my body was limber. I could go like the wind, if necessary. Others weren't so lucky. I felt sorry for those who weren't nimble-footed and spry. They had a rough time. There was my 180-pound neighbor-in-formation. She'd manage to arrive at the right place at the right time, but always a-huffin' and a-puffin'. She lost ten pounds the first week.

It was impossible to be bored. We didn't have time. Even during rest periods, we were likely to be lined up someplace to be marched somewhere, perhaps to be issued something: another pair of drawers, a gas mask, that new item of underwear — Vests, WAAC 2 (khaki, of course).

Usually, we had the same activity at the same time each day. But occasionally the special nature of an activity required a deviation from the daily routine. Like the day we had gas mask drill instead of physical training. With the straps of the canvas bags on our right shoulders and across our bodies so the gas masks would rest on our left hips, we marched one squad at a time to an immense field I had never seen before. About fifty feet from the path stood a small concrete building. Notwithstanding the absence of windows, I assumed it was a latrine, two rows of four doubles. Aside from mentally complimenting the army for its efficiency and thoughtfulness, I gave it no more thought.

Lieutenant Bolton was saying, "We're going to learn how to put on our gas masks so that in the event you should ever find yourself in a situation where you will need it, you will be able to get it on without any hesitation."

I began to get nervous. I was nimble as a rabbit with the feet, but clumsy as hell with the hands.

I watched her very closely as she said, "Now listen carefully, and do as I do. First, remove your gas mask from around your neck and hold it in your hands. Now — hold your gas mask case in your left hand, and, on the count of 'one,' place the strap around your neck, like this," and she put the strap over her right shoulder so the gas mask came to rest on the left hip.

"That's exactly how you had it before, right? Ready
. . . ONE!" There was a bustle of activity as the arms
moved to encircle the necks with the straps. The
Lieutenant looked around. "Good," she said. "Now
on the count of 'two,' unbuckle the case like this . . .
TWO! Fine. On 'three,' remove the mask with your
right hand . . . THREE! Good. On 'four,' place the
mask over the face . . . FOUR!"

I was still unbuckling.

"Blumenthal, what's the trouble?"

"My buckle is stuck, ma'am."

She came over to help me. "Just press this little
thing and it will slide right out."

"Yes, ma'am."

"Now take out the mask — good — now on the
face — fine."

She looked over the group. "That looks good," she
said. "Remove your mask and put it back in the case.
We'll do it again, this time by the numbers. You do
each of the steps as I call the numbers one to four.
Ready?"

One! . . . TWO! . . . THREE! . . . FOUR! . . .

I was still unbuckling.

"Blumenthal, you'll have to do some practicing in
the barracks."

"Yes, ma'am." Again she helped me.

"Now remove your mask again," she said to the
group, "and put it back in the bag. This last time I will
just call 'Gas!' Get your masks on as quickly as you
can."

Needless to say, everyone else had crossed the

finish line when I was just coming round the first bend. By the time I was ready to put my mask on, my face was so red, I was happy to cover it.

Lieutenant Bolton checked everyone to make certain her gas mask was properly in place. When she had completed the inspection, once more she addressed the group. "Now listen to me carefully," she said. "You will line up one behind the other. Do you see that building?" she asked, pointing to the concrete latrine. "You are going to enter that building one person at a time."

"But I don't have to go," I felt like telling her.

"One of you will go inside," she continued, "and the next one in line will go up to the door and wait so that she can enter as soon as the woman ahead of her has emerged. When you get inside, close the door quickly behind you, count slowly to ten, and then come out, closing the door quickly again."

But surely she was joking. Surely she didn't mean that it was not a latrine, but that inside that building was a heavy concentration of real gas — the kind that kills. No, no, they wouldn't take that chance. Yet, why did she say "Close the door quickly behind you"? Why did she say "Count to ten" only — why not one hundred? How could I be sure my gas mask had been carefully inspected?

I was fourth in line. My turn came. My feet were two pieces of lead cemented to the ground. It didn't matter that two women had already come bouncing jauntily out, apparently enjoying the best of health. My feet wouldn't move.

"Blumenthal, get up there. You're next."

Someone must have given me a shove, for suddenly I was right outside the concrete building. A masked young lady emerged and said blithely, "It's all yours." Once more, my feet wouldn't move, so I must have gotten a second shove, for there I was — inside. I had no choice but to close the door behind me. I took a deep breath, counted "Two-four-six-eight-ten," then quickly opened the door, closed it behind me, and exhaled.

"You're a fast counter," said the WAAC waiting outside the door.

"That's the way we count in New Jersey," I answered. "And if you think I count fast, watch me run," I called over my shoulder as I galloped away from the building and back to the squad.

We suffered no casualties, I'm happy to report — a credit to Lieutenant Bolton's fine instruction and to information I subsequently received. Not only could we have counted to one hundred without danger, we could have sat down and had a game of bridge. Inside that lethal concrete building, was — you guessed it — a heavy concentration of good, clean air.

During the fourth and last week of basic training, an excitement pervaded the barracks — an excitement comprising anticipation, suspense, and the uneasiness that accompanies uncertainty. In a few days, we would be dispersed, severing permanently the ties we had developed over this four-week period, leaving the security of the barracks and the people in them we had come to know so well, shielded no more by the protective wings of the officers we had come to regard as our guardians in our home away from home. It meant going out into the cold unknown for training to replace male soldiers and eventually scattering to the four corners of the United States Army.

In the evening hours of this last week, most of our conversation centered on possible assignments and our preferences for these assignments. At this early stage in the life of the Women's Army Auxiliary Corps, only four training programs had been implemented. The possibilities for assignment were:

1. COOKS AND BAKERS SCHOOL. This program was the least popular. Most people to whom I talked had not been inspired one iota by the cooks they had seen in our mess hall, standing behind titanic cauldrons adding twelve pounds of salt to a stew; or by the bakers they had seen removing a thousand breakfast rolls coinstantaneously from the gigantic ovens. Trudy expressed it quite succinctly for most of us. "I'll kill myself," she said.

2. CADRE. This was the second lowest in popularity. It meant being assigned to a WAAC basic training company to become an assistant to the company officers, taking over such duties as close order drill, clerical work, and issuance of supplies to trainees. This appealed to some of the women because it meant training could be accomplished on the job, eliminating formal classroom work and involvement in lectures, studying, and tests.

3. MOTOR POOL. This was quite popular, maybe because it seemed like a good way of getting around

and going places. I think most of those who wanted to be assigned to the motor pool envisioned themselves opening the door for and saluting a five-star General. Those who were fortunate enough to get the assignment soon learned, to their deep chagrin, that the army had more garbage that needed driving than five-star Generals. (For men, hauling the garbage turned out to be one of the most desirable jobs; these jobholders were not released for active duty by a WAAC. The women were not allowed to haul the garbage, only to drive it.)

4. ADMINISTRATION SCHOOL. Not only was administration school the most popular of the available assignments, it was the most prestigious. A four-week course produced an administrative specialist equipped to handle the multitudinous paperwork required in the army. It prepared cadre to be experts formally trained in the duties of First Sergeant, Supply Sergeant, and Company Clerk. We speculated that only those with the highest qualifications would be selected to go to administration school. This assignment would give one stature. It would indicate one was really somebody.

Naturally, my preference was for Administration School. There was no question in my mind but that it would be my assignment. I had become familiar with the backgrounds of many of the WAACs in my company, and I was aware that mine was as good as any. With this knowledge, I felt no apprehension about my qualifications for this exalted assignment.

On the last day of basic training, which was also

the day we were to get our orders, everybody was keyed up. We sat on our stripped beds, barracks bags alongside packed to the hilt. We made meaningless conversation, bit our nails, and watched the doorway.

When Lieutenant Bolton made her first appearance, the WAAC nearest the door called, "Attention!" and we all jumped to our feet. "At ease," said Lieutenant Bolton. "I'll be appearing and reappearing, so you may remain seated until your name is called."

At ten-minute intervals, she appeared in the doorway, called a few names, then disappeared out the door with several over-the-shoulder barracks-bag-laden WAACs in tow.

The number of those left in the barracks was getting smaller and smaller, and I was getting sicker and sicker. By the time only four of us were left, I had chewed my nails down to the first knuckle.

Lieutenant Bolton appeared again. My heart was pumping and my eyelids were jumping. I thought she would never speak. A year and a half later, she spoke. "You four auxiliaries will be assigned to WAAC companies as cadre," she said, and then she told us where to go. And I would have liked to have been able to tell her where she could go.

I was crushed. I couldn't believe it. How could they do this to me? How could they make me another pipe-fitter-turned-sleeve-setter? I felt utterly humiliated. Was this a precursor of things to come? Was it to be my destiny in the army to have a career which failed to take notice that I was capable of at least a scintilla of cerebral activity? Where had I gone wrong? Were my ambitions tremendously unrealistic? I didn't think so. It wasn't as though I was still twelve years old, when my greatest ambition had been to be a Park Avenue call girl.

The other three women had left, and I sat on my bed in the empty squadroom indulging my bitterness and fighting back the tears. When the shadows began to creep into the room, I knew I had no choice but to go to my new assignment. Flinging my barracks bags over my shoulders, I made my way to my new station — one flight down. I had been assigned as cadre to this very same company.

When I reached my sleeping quarters, my spirits lifted a little. Each barracks building had a cadre room at the far end of the downstairs squadroom. It was made to accommodate two persons, but since I was the only cadre assigned to this platoon, I would have the room to myself. It wasn't much of a room. It was about eight feet by ten feet and had two beds, two footlockers, and two wall lockers. There wasn't much space to move around in, but after four weeks of living in public, this was the pinnacle of luxury. I had my very own four walls at which I could stare, and my very own door which I could open and close to admit or shut out the babble, and — even more important — in four short weeks of living in the army, I was able to achieve what I had failed to accomplish in a lifetime of living at home: a room of my own.

The babble had already commenced. Although the beds were hardly cold, a new WAAC company was being brought in to occupy them. I stood unnoticed in the doorway for a moment and watched the new trainees as they arrived and threw their suitcases on their beds. It was my arrival scene four weeks earlier: the same three-inch heels, the same pillbox hats, the same smartly tailored suits and coats, the same confused faces, and the same conversation: "Hi. I'm Alice." "My God! This is it?" "Where are you from?" "I must have been out of my mind." One woman named Bette said, "What a dump!"

I stepped into the squadroom. Someone spotted me and stopped talking. One by one, they saw me, and the room became soundless. My spirits lifted a little higher. I had the power to hush a room. In one brief moment, by virtue of wearing a WAAC uniform among a group of civilian-clad women, I had achieved greatness. I walked to the middle of the room and introduced myself. I explained that I was there to work with and to help them. They surrounded me, plying me with questions, and my spirits soared. Four weeks of basic training made me a seasoned veteran among a bunch of rookies. In one short month, I had completed a meteoric climb to stardom.

After these stature-building moments, I wasn't very surprised to discover I liked my work. I and the other two acting noncoms assigned to our company not only assisted the company officers with their duties, we took over many of them. We accompanied the officers on inspection tours; we took the platoons out on the drill field; we made ourselves available to the trainees for whatever help they might need. The recruits called me "Sarge" and came to me with their problems; they had great respect for the infinite wisdom I had accumulated in the four weeks during which they were still civilians.

After one week as an acting noncommissioned officer, I was glad I had received this assignment. I was really enjoying it. To make things even better, I was flattered when, in the supply room one day, I overheard a conversation taking place in the orderly room next door. Lieutenant Bentley (who had replaced Peter) was saying to Lieutenant Simon, one of the WAAC platoon commanders, "You know Blumenthal from the first platoon? I watched her drill her platoon this morning. She barks out her commands like an experienced drill sergeant and gives them on the correct foot every time. Never misses. She's great."

I swelled with pride and was ready to stay there for the duration. How lucky I was not to have been sent to Administration School!

Two days later, I received orders for Administration School.

CHAPTER FIFTEEN

White Tablecloths In The Sunset

Like so many other hotels all over the country during the war, the Hotel Savery in downtown Des Moines had been commandeered by the United States government for use as an army installation. It lent itself quite effectively to the purpose for which it had been appropriated — to house the Women's Army Auxiliary Corps School of Administration. The bedrooms became administrative offices for the several WAAC companies that would be in the hotel at one time and also living quarters for the WAAC officers. The public rooms — dining rooms and banquet halls — became squadrooms and classrooms.

In this hotel I was to begin the studies that would transform me into an administrative specialist. I had mixed emotions about my transfer. On one hand, this assignment had been my first choice, and it gave me a sense of gratification; on the other, once more I was just a small cog, and I had rather enjoyed being a big wheel. The transfer had removed my position of prominence, my prestige, and my privacy, all of which had served to restore a feeling of importance.

We were seventy-eight in the company this time, all bedded in one room — a room that had probably been used formerly for small family weddings. It was arranged with three rows of double-deckers, thirteen to a row, with room to walk between the beds if we walked sideways. Even then, if we weren't careful we'd knock down our clothing, which hung on three hangers per WAAC on the sides of the bed, lower occupant on the right, upper occupant on the left. Only GI clothing was allowed; we had no wall lockers, so all civilian clothes had to go into the barracks bag, under the mattress, or home. Because of these close quarters, we found ourselves ambulating only when certain functions required us to. It was less wear and tear on our bodies and tempers to stay put on our beds. In effect, our squadroom became a squatroom.

Sleeping in the upper story of a duplex bed is not exactly what I would have chosen, in view of my nocturnal acrobatics and recollections of nights when an overambitious maneuver had flipped me right onto the floor. That first night I was afraid to move, lest I move one inch too many. I concluded that trying to sleep "at attention" wasn't all that much fun. In fact, I didn't sleep at all. Once I dozed off for a moment only to awake in terror, having dreamed I had turned over and off the bed and hurtled down, down, down into a mysterious and frightening bottomless darkness.

But everything was better after that first night. I traded beds with my downstairs neighbor. I gave her a carton of cigarettes for the lower level and offered to throw in the mineral oil, but she said, "No, thanks. The cigarettes will do just fine."

Administration school was rough, but it was a different kind of regimen from basic training. In basic, the activity had been largely physical. Here it was a steady grind of attendance at classes and studying. Our accelerated four-week course, commonly referred to as "the blitz," was designed to provide the women's army with much-needed administrative specialists to staff WAAC companies and other WAAC administrative offices.

We received a book called *Company Administration Including Supply and Mess Management and Personnel Records Including Personnel Office Organization and Procedure*, written by, so help me, Lieutenant Colonel C.M. *Virtue*, Infantry, U.S. Army — no relation to Colonel Don *Faith*, Commandant, Fort Des Moines, Iowa.

It was no picnic. We were blitzed with forms and abbreviations, numbers of copies, dispositions of copies, inclusions and exclusions, abbreviations and forms, authorized and unauthorized activities, authorized and unauthorized expenditures, authorized unauthorizations, unauthorized authorizations, and forms and abbreviations.

That was the first day.

Then we learned that "daily strength for rations" had nothing to do with the army's solicitude for our physical capacity for food intake, but was instead a record of the number of persons eating with the company, used as a basis for the amount of food to be provided. We also learned that "men messing separate-ly" did not refer to the GIs' sex habits but was the term used for men authorized to eat in places other than their own companies. The Morning Report, we dis-covered, was not a report by pregnant wives on their morning sickness but was a twenty-page booklet in which was recorded the daily history of the company with all changes affecting any member.

There were numbers assigned to the papers and reports — all of which we had to know. The Morning Report, for instance, was W.D. AGO Form #1; it was authorized by AR 345-400 and was not to be confused with W.D. IGD Form #1, authorized by AR 20-35, the Inventory and Inspection Report, prepared in duplicate and used for the disposition of all items of supply except public animals, which were prepared on W.D. IGD Form #2 (AR 20-35, par. 3), except horses, which were prepared on W.D. IGD Form #3 (AR 20-35, par. 4).

The W.D. QMC Form #445 was used for overages, shortages, and damages, and was aptly named the Over, Short, and Damaged Report. For instance, a Company Commander might be charged on his Memorandum Receipt (authorized by CIR 105, W.D. 1942) with 175 pillows, feather, and have signed a receipt for such items. On a detailed physical invento-ry of his property, he discovers that 23 of these pillows are not feather at all but cotton, and that of the remaining 152, the feathers in 4 are flying all over the goddamned place. So he prepares W.D. QMC Form #445, the Over, Short, and Damaged Report, and lists as follows:

Pillows, cotton — over   23

Pillows, feather — short   23

Pillows, feather — damaged   4

When the Women's Army Auxiliary Corps was activated, many new forms were developed (no pun intended). It was only natural that this should be so. Just as the clothing had to be changed, and the latrines at old Fort Des Moines had to undergo a facelift (although a different part of the anatomy might better describe the alteration), so did some of the paperwork. Yet somebody must have recognized that the old W.D. QMC Form #445 would adequately cover at least one new situation. On a Monday morning, after all her women had returned from their weekend passes, a Company Commander could make a capsulized report to higher echelons as follows:

WAACs — over   None

WAACs — short   None

WAACs — damaged   Four

The authorized abbreviations drove us crazy. Four hundred sixty of them were listed in Colonel Virtue's book. I have no recollection of how many we had to memorize. I only remember that, far into the night, long after "lights out," on each of thirty-eight double-decker beds, two flashlights — one up, one down — made eerie rings of light throughout the darkness of the room. Like a religious chant, seventy-eight voices intoned: "E-M-B Embarkation; E-P-T-E Existed Prior to Enlistment; E-G Expert Gunner; E-R Expert Rifleman; E-T-S Expiration of Term of Service;

E-A-D Extended Active Duty," ad infinitum, ad nause-
um. On and on we warbled, until, by morning, we
were in a drunken stupor of whirling abbreviations.
HP-Y N YR!

Everybody griped, naturally. We griped at the
army for using abbreviations; we griped at the officers
for making us memorize the abbreviations; we griped
at Colonel Virtue for putting them into his book.
Taking it out on the good Colonel was really quite
unfair, although I doubt the Colonel cared a hoot. At
$1.95 a copy, Virtue had his own reward.

During the week, we had little time for anything
but our studies. On weekends, however, we emerged
from our confinement. I enjoyed Des Moines. It was
a stimulating change to get away from the sand and
gravel of the fort and into the soot and grime of the
city. Snapping pictures was our favorite pastime, and
the State Capitol our favorite snapping place. Between
the pictures taken during our four-week basic training
weekends and those we took during this four-week
period, I have snapshots of myself in uniform on every
step of the Capitol building. In the ones showing me
in my belted utility coat leaning against the lamppost
in front of the Capitol building, I look like Agent
Double 0 waiting for her contact. When we weren't
taking pictures, we strolled past the expensive shops
again to do our window shopping and past the expensive restaurants to do our window eating.

One afternoon during my second week at the
hotel, I was resting on my bed after the last class of the
day and before mess. I received word that I had a

visitor in the lobby. I rushed downstairs to find Peter. Could I have dinner with him? Oh, boy, could I! I flew upstairs to get permission from the acting First Sergeant, who zoomed downstairs to get me a pass from the Company Commander, and I floated off into the sunset to enjoy the luxury of Peter, a filet mignon, and gadzooks! a white tablecloth.

The four weeks went by, the blitz was over at last, and once more we received orders. Mine read:

RESTRICTED
Headquarters,

First Women's Army Auxiliary Corps Training Center	
Transfer Memorandum	Fort Des Moines, Iowa
Number 28	November 14, 1942

EXTRACT

1. The follg chgs in asgmt and dy are drctd, eff this date:

Rose Blumenthal A 304062 fr Co.7, 2nd Rgt

to Co. 9 3rd Rgt to rpt to CC as cadre

English translation:

Fort Des Moines, here I come,

Right back where I started from.

Actually, I wasn't exactly right back where I started from. I was an acting Platoon Sergeant again, but with a difference. Four weeks of secondary education had placed me one rung above those directly out of basic training and had removed me from the ranks of the untrained cadre.

During the first two weeks out of Administration School, I moved up fast on the ladder of success. At the end of one week, the Supply Sergeant was transferred out unexpectedly (like there's any other way in the army), and I was promoted to acting Supply Sergeant. This new job was indeed quite appropriate, for I had the finest qualifications. I had made history in administration school with a score of ninety-two correct answers out of a possible ninety-three. Now this outstanding performance would stand me in good stead. I could tell you at the snap of a falling dish that if an article of public property was lost or damaged by the fault of any officer or enlisted person, that person would be required to pay the value thereof as shown in current price lists, or the cost of repairs in such amounts as might be determined by a Report of Survey, and that for this purpose a statement of Charges, W.D. AGD Form #36, should be used as authorized by par. 2, AR 35 6640.

As Supply Sergeant, I ordered the office and barracks supplies. I prepared requisitions for clothing and equipment for the newly arrived recruits and supervised their issue. I listened to their gripes that a blouse was too big or a skirt too short.

I was on this job for one week when the acting First Sergeant was transferred out (unexpectedly of course), and I was promoted to acting First Sergeant.

Now I had really arrived. Not only did I have a certificate, I also had a whistle. One shrill blast from this glorious hunk of tin and I could watch with amazement as three buildings discharged a sprinting mass of 150 falling, stumbling, pushing new recruits responding to my call, fighting to get into some kind of military order before I called in my most authoritarian Sergeant voice, "Atten-SHUN!" I couldn't help but remember that in the not-too-distant past I had been a stumbling, pushing recruit, and, despite my exquisite intoxication with power, I felt compassion — the kind of compassion one feels when one passes a motorist on the road changing a tire and one thinks, "Poor devil — but better you than I."

As First Sergeant, I had a full day. Before breakfast, I'd grope my way to the orderly room to get started with my work; if the completed Morning Report authorized by AR 345-400 was not in Battalion Headquarters by 0900 hours, there'd be hell to pay (authorized by the 104th Article of War), and in the "Incidents" section of the Morning Report, directly under "Aux. Evans goes sick in hospital with mumps at 0800 hours," there would be a second entry: "Aux. Blumenthal, acting First Sergeant, gets axe at 0930 hours."

At the proper time, I'd go out into the black outdoors and blow my whistle. I formed the company, conducted roll call, about-faced and saluted and presented the company to my Company Commander, who was still buckling her garter. She presented the company back to me, and I marched my charges and my growling stomach to breakfast.

Back in the orderly room after mess there was the Morning Report to finish, the daily Sick Report to prepare, duty rosters, instructions to the Company Clerk, instructions to the Company Commander, inspection tours, gig sheets, and drill. There was so much to do that frequently I'd come back after evening mess to finish my work. I didn't mind. In fact, I enjoyed it. These evenings gave me an opportunity to become acquainted with many of the women in the company, for during those hours I'd make myself available to them for the nostalgias that needed nursing and the axes that needed grinding. If it weren't for the nostalgias and the axes, I wouldn't have known most of the trainees except as snappy pairs of eyes right. There was Henrietta, for instance, who wanted her bed changed to be near Helen, and Helen, who wanted her squadroom changed to get away from Henrietta. There was Carol, who asked to be excused from physical training because she didn't feel well this time of month. She was the one who, in high school, always had this time of month on gym days.

I always tried to be sympathetic and helpful. When Barbara came into the orderly room with tears in her eyes and said, "I don't know what to do. I pull and I pull and I pull, and my corners come out round," I suggested she get her neighbor to yank while she pulled; and when Jean asked me what to do because she gets homesick a lot, what could I tell her but to do what the other gals do when they get homesick a lot, and that was to cry a lot. Both women came in the following day to thank me. Barbara told me she and her neighbor pulled and yanked so hard they tore the sheet, but she was able to hide it under the blanket; Jean said she went back to the barracks and sobbed and sobbed and sobbed, and with everybody telling her to shut up, she got to know a lot of people and wasn't homesick anymore.

There was also Marty, an adorable little pixie from Indiana who made a perfect bed, who had no nostalgias that needed nursing and no axes to grind, and who took physical training every day. She would just stick her head in the doorway and say, "Hi."

The one I remember best was Terry. She came into the orderly room the very first evening she arrived, still in her civilian clothes. I said to this pretty lass with the round, cherubic face, guileless eyes, and magnificent hair to her shoulders — red, I think, "Won't you sit down?"

"Oh, thank you," she answered as she sat. "I thought you might like some chocolate," she continued, handing me a Hershey chocolate bar.

"Thank you," I said. I loved chocolate bars. "What's your name?"

"Theresa Peasly. But please call me Terry."

"All right. Where are you from, Terry?"

"Kansas City."

"I see. That was very thoughtful of you to stop by with a Hershey bar for me."

"Won't you have another?" She held one toward me. "You can save it for later, if you like."

"All right. But that's all. First thing you know, my uniform won't fit me."

"Sergeant, if I look half as well in my uniform as you look in yours, I'll be happy."

"You will," I lied. I had noticed she had a pretty fat bottom.

The next night she came again. This time the Hershey bars had nuts. She developed the habit of dropping in every night with the chocolate bars, sometimes with nuts and sometimes without. I couldn't help wondering whether she had ordered a host of porters to carry her chocolate-filled luggage when she entrained, or whether she had a standing order with a Des Moines store to be supplied daily.

"You have no idea how much this means to me," Terry said one night, "to have someone intelligent to talk to."

"Well, it's nice having you," and your Hershey bars, I might have added.

One night Terry came in just as I had finished the duty roster for the following week.

"What kind tonight?" I asked.

"With nuts."

"Oh, good." My mouth full of chocolate, I said to Terry, "I just got through writing your name. You're coming up for KP again."

"Oh?"

I looked at the duty roster not yet posted. "On Tuesday."

"I guess it'll be all right."

"What do you mean you guess it'll be all right? Is something wrong?"

"Not really. It's just that the last time I was on KP, I got a little rash on my hand."

"Did you go on sick call?"

"Oh, no. I didn't want to miss anything. I figured I was just allergic to all that soap. It was nothing. It went away in a few days."

"If you're really worried about it, I can give you CQ. Would you like that?"

"Oh, could you?"

"Of course. You'll have CQ next Tuesday," I said,

scratching her name from the KP list.

"You really are the greatest," she said, and I almost scratched her name from CQ. She was such a charming woman!

And I was such an innocent lamb!

During this time, when I was acting First Sergeant with Company Nine, an old problem returned to torment me. Several weeks earlier, classes had opened for Officer Candidate School for WAACs from the ranks, and many were applying and being accepted. Once more I faced the perplexing question — should I or shouldn't I? It wasn't that I was still possessed by those old unrealistic fears. Long since dissipated was my image of the WAAC officer as an omniscient being, a paragon of virtue, strength, and brilliance. But now I had new unrealistic fears.

Rumors had reached us that the failure rate at OCS was astronomical, sometimes reaching as high as 50 percent. Maybe this was an exaggeration, but, true or not, the prospect of failing was frightening. Nobody likes to fail, true. But nobody hated to fail worse than I did. To me, "washing out" of OCS was an unthinkable ignominy difficult to reconcile with living thereafter. What would I do? Nothing rash, of course. I'd simply crawl away to some deep and inaccessible hole and die of shame.

My paralyzing neuroses were threatening to keep me inexorably committed to a whistle. Until one day, in a moment of magnificent strength, I took hold of myself and said, "Rose, you are a fool."

That did it. Nobody talks to me that way. I'd have

packed right then and there, except in order to attend OCS, it was necessary to apply and be accepted. That very day, I obtained an application blank, completed it, and sent it off. It was done!

Prior to this time, I had been contemplating requesting a furlough for a visit home. After filing my application for OCS, I learned that the next class would start some time in February. It was still early January, so I had ample time to take a furlough and get back in time even if I was accepted for the next class. I applied and received a ten-day furlough due to start on January 22 and end on February 1.

The night before I left I had a date with Peter. We drove into Des Moines and found a small Italian restaurant complete with candlelight and red-checked tablecloths.

We ate a lot, talked a lot, and laughed a lot. We also had an extra laugh from an unexpected source. Seated at a neighboring table were seven persons, including a little boy I judged to be about four years old. Peter and I had finished dinner and were waiting for the check when a young lady en route to another table recognized an acquaintance, who happened to be the mother of the four-year-old, and stopped to chat. During a lull in our conversation, Peter and I couldn't help overhearing part of theirs.

Said the mother, "What kind of dog do you have?"

"It's a cocker spaniel," answered the visiting lady.

"Is it male or female?" asked the mother.

"It's female."

At this point in the conversation, the four-year-old

interrupted with "Mommy, what's a female?"

Mommy answered, "A girl's a female. And a boy's a male. Like, you're a male and daddy's a male. Understand?"

"Yes, Mommy, I understand," answered the youngster. "I'm a male and Daddy's a male and you're a cocker spaniel."

Everybody laughed, of course.

"Lucky thing the mother's young and pretty," I said, chuckling. "If she hadn't been, she might not have laughed so hard."

"You mean at being called a cocker spaniel?"

"Right."

"I see what you mean. I guess being called a dog is as bad as being called an old bag. Say . . . I have a riddle."

"I hate riddles."

"Are you ready?"

"I guess I have no choice. Ready."

"If an old, ugly woman is called an old bag, what would you call an old, ugly dog?"

"I give up."

"A doggie bag."

"Ugh. I hate puns even worse than I hate riddles."

"You'll have to admit, I'm fast."

"Oh, that you are — not good, but fast."

"In fact, I'm the fastest pun-slinger in the Midwest."

"That does it," I said. "Take me home."

"Why? Just because you don't like puns?"

"No — because I told you I'd have to leave early to pack. I leave tomorrow. Remember?"

CHAPTER SIXTEEN

Not All Soldiers
Wear Pants

At Pennsylvania Station in Newark, New Jersey, I had a joyful reunion with sister Miriam and brother Jack, husband of sister-in-law Ethel (not to be confused with brother-in-law Jack, husband of sister Miriam). I was very glad Miriam had come to meet me; I was anxious to tell her the big news that I had applied to Officer Candidate School and that, if accepted, I would probably "wash out." I believe in softening the blow.

Back home, sundry relatives gathered to bid me welcome, the same sundry relatives plus one who had gathered together to bid me adieu. The plus one was Jay, who had been the pregnant part of sister-in-law Helen, four months earlier. Everybody was excited about the uniform, including Jay, who wanted to eat the shiny buttons.

My brother Joe said, "It looks great!"

Niece Mildred said, "Super!"

Niece Lucille said, "Terrif!"

Sister Anne said, "Probably cost $22.75" (she owned a women's apparel shop).

My mother said, "Your uniform looks good, but you don't look so good. You're so skinny. Are you eating enough?

I spent a hectic week. I was visited by friends and relatives, and I visited friends, relatives, and the new tenant downstairs, to whom my mother had made a promise to show me in the flesh.

I didn't stay at home for the entire furlough. Prior to leaving the fort, I had decided that, for a change of pace, I would spend a few days at a vacation resort before returning to camp. From home I called the Woods Hotel, about fifty miles out of New York City.

"Your name, please?" asked the reservation clerk on the phone.

"Sergeant Rose Blumenthal," I answered. Use of the noncommissioned officer rank now came naturally to me. I was accustomed to being called "Sergeant," even though the WAAC Table of Organization had still not been finalized and WAAC stripes were not yet dispensed. Besides, suppose I had said, "Auxiliary Blumenthal." The clerk would have thought either that I was out of my mind or that I was a member of a ladies' organization connected with the local hospital.

"We'll expect you on Tuesday," said the clerk.

Next I called my friend Dorothy, who lived in New York. I had written telling her that I was coming home and expressed the hope that I could see her on Friday night. I was planning to spend the night before returning to Des Moines at a hotel in New York City.

"Will I see you on Friday night?" I asked Dorothy after we had exchanged greetings.

"Didn't you get my letter?" she asked. "I'm leaving for the West Coast tomorrow morning for a visit home."

"Oh. Rotten timing. I'm disappointed."

"So am I. But listen. Under no circumstances are you to stay at a hotel. You'll spend Friday night at my apartment. I'll leave the key with the doorman. There'll be some food in the fridge, and there's a little grocery store around the corner if you want to pick up a couple of things."

"OK. Maybe I'll do that."

"Sorry I won't get to see you."

"Maybe next time. Have a good trip, and thanks for the apartment."

Leaving home was a little less sorrowful this time. I promised to take care of myself. I promised to write. I promised to eat everything. I promised not to get court-martialed. And I promised to send more pictures.

I arrived at the Woods Hotel late Tuesday afternoon. I rested for a while, then showered, dressed, and came down to dinner. In the doorway of the attractive dining room, I stopped. The maitre d' hotel hurried to greet me.

"How do you do," he said graciously, but looking rather surprised as he examined the paper on the clipboard. "May I have your name, please?"

"Blumenthal."

"Not Sergeant Blumenthal!"

"Yes."

He looked startled. "Oh. I thought — er — that is . . ."

"That I was a man?"

"Why, yes. I'm sorry. There's no first name here."

"Well — no harm done."

"Oh, no. Of course not. Come with me, please."

He led me to a table at which sat a man about forty-five, his attractive blonde wife, and their two daughters. The older daughter looked about twenty and wore her blonde hair in an upsweep. The younger one was dark and looked about fourteen.

"This is Sergeant Blumenthal," said the maitre d'. "Dr. and Mrs. Stone, and Carol," nodding towards the older young lady, "and Susan."

"How do you do," we all said together; that is, almost all of us said it together. I noticed that Carol was speechless, her mouth and her eyes wide open.

She's awed by the uniform, I thought. There aren't many WAACs around. Maybe I'm the first one she's seen. I must make a special effort to be friendly and put her at ease.

The Stone family were warm people and made pleasant conversation. They asked many questions about the Women's Army Auxiliary Corps.

"I understand you'll be part of the army soon," said Dr. Stone.

"That's right. We'll drop the 'auxiliary.' We'll be WAC — Women's Army Corps."

Mrs. Stone asked, "Will it be mandatory for you to stay in at the time of the changeover?"

"No. We'll have the option of getting a discharge at

that time. Those who choose to stay in will be sworn into the United States Army."

"Are you planning to stay in?"

"Oh, yes."

"I suppose being part of the army will give you many advantages," said Dr. Stone.

"Yes. We'll have the same benefits as GIs — the same salaries, the same educational benefits and dependency allotments, and we'll even have free postage."

"None of which you have now."

"No. Our rank titles will change, too."

"Rank titles?" Dr. Stone look puzzled.

I explained how our titles would be the same as those of the men — the noncommissioned officers would be Corporals and Sergeants instead of Junior Leaders and First Leaders.

Carol said almost nothing during the entire meal.

"Carol," I said, "think you'd like to be a WAAC?" Not brilliant, but a start.

"No, thanks. Mother, may I be excused?"

"Yes, you may."

"Me, too, Mom?" asked Susan.

After both girls had left, Mrs. Stone said, "I hope you'll excuse me too. I promised to play bridge at eight o'clock, and I'm late already." She rose, gave her husband a peck on the cheek, said, "I'll see you later," and left.

After Mrs. Stone had gone, Dr. Stone said, "Can you keep a secret?"

"Of course."

"How old do you think Carol is?" he asked.

"I would guess about twenty."

"She's seventeen."

"Oh. She looks older."

"Let me tell you what happened. But please, never let on I told you. At lunch today, the maitre d' came over to us and said a Sergeant was checking in this afternoon and that he would seat the young man at our table."

"The office didn't give him my first name. He assumed I was a man."

"Carol lit up like a Christmas tree."

"Oh, no."

"She went upstairs right after lunch, cold-creamed her face, rested, and then spent hours getting her hair in the upsweep. She usually wears it down to her shoulders."

"Oh, dear."

"That isn't all. She wore her best dress, borrowed her mother's turquoise earrings, and practically drowned herself in her mother's Chanel Number 5. When the maitre d' introduced you as the Sergeant, I thought she was going into shock."

"And I thought she was awed by the uniform. Actually, she loathed it. The bottom half was all wrong. Not all soldiers wear pants."

Dr. Stone laughed. "That's right. But don't worry about it. She'll get over it. Youth is resilient."

We walked out of the dining room together. In the lobby, Carol was sitting off in a corner by herself.

"Why don't I go over and talk to Carol? Do you

think she'll chew me up?"

"I don't know. But go ahead, if you like. I'll see you later."

I walked over to where Carol was sitting in the corner of the sofa looking miserable.

"Mind if I sit down?" I asked.

"I don't care. Do as you please." Hardly an auspicious beginning.

"Would you like to go for a walk?" I asked.

"No, thank you."

We sat for a few moments without speaking.

"You know, Carol," I ventured, "I guess things would be a lot more interesting here if there were a few unattached men around."

There. That would show her we had a common meeting ground — that we shared a problem.

"No such luck," she answered. "All the nineteen-year-old boys are in the service."

Well, that took care of me. To Carol, the dating world was made up only of seventeen-year-old girls and nineteen-year-old boys. Anybody twenty years old or over was antediluvian and certainly couldn't be interested in persons of the opposite sex.

But I don't give up easily. "I guess things can get pretty dull for a girl without boys around to date."

"Didn't you think it was dull if you didn't have boys to date when you were a girl?" she asked.

Watch it, kid. No trouble at all for me to rip those gorgeous, big turquoise earrings right off those beautiful pink little ears.

But what was I thinking of? She was just a child.

"Come on, Carol," I said. "Keep your chin up. The war will be over soon, and all the boys will be back home. In the meantime, keep busy with other things. You can do it. I can tell. You look like a gal who has lots of pluck."

"Oh, I suppose you're right," she conceded. "I guess I'm being pretty selfish. Here you are in uniform serving your country, and I'm complaining about boys and dates."

Ha. I was getting to her.

"I really do admire you," she continued. "You're the one with pluck. Just getting old without letting yourself get depressed takes pluck."

Well, pluck you, sister. That did it. I left.

I spent the next couple of days pleasantly — eating, reading, walking, and avoiding Carol. On Friday afternoon, I left the hotel for New York City and Dorothy's apartment.

CHAPTER SEVENTEEN

Potato Chips Are Nice, Too

At the apartment house where Dorothy lived in mid-Manhattan, a door on the street led into a small vestibule about eight by ten feet. A second door opened into the lobby. When the doorman gave me Dorothy's key, he told me he was on duty only until 11:30, and that when he left at that time, he locked the inside door. He explained that the street door remained unlocked, but that if I was planning to go out and to return after 11:30, it would be necessary to use the apartment key to get into the lobby.

I thanked the doorman and went up on the elevator to the third floor and Dorothy's attractive orange-and-brown sofa-bed apartment. It was late afternoon, and I napped for a while on the brown sofa under the orange afghan, then freshened up and went out. I bought a newspaper, found a small French restaurant in the neighborhood, read my paper, and dawdled over dinner. When I was through, it was only nine o'clock, so I decided to go to a movie. En route to the restaurant, I had seen two movie houses and noted their pictures. My choices were between Buster Crabbe in *Tarzan, the Fearless* or Johnny Weismuller in *Tarzan's New York Adventure*. Because I hadn't seen either, and because I never could tell the difference between Buster Crabbe and Johnny Weismuller, I did it the easy way and went into the theater I passed first on the way back. To this day I don't know which picture I saw, except I remember that Boy was snatched by a circus man.

What with the newsreels and the movie shorts and the short shorts and getting Boy back, it was almost midnight by the time I returned to the apartment building. I opened the street door, walked across the small vestibule, and inserted the key into the lock of the inside door. Just as I opened the door, I heard the street door open. I turned to see a man entering. I decided I would not be like the unfriendly New Yorker who didn't know his next-door neighbor; I would hold open the door for this neighbor so he wouldn't need to go into his pocket for his key. I gave him a friendly, neighborly smile as he took the door from me, and we walked to the elevator together. When we reached it, I pressed the button.

The elevator was going up, and it went all the way to the tenth floor. As we waited in silence for it to descend, I began to get that strange feeling of being stared at. At first I ignored it, but when I began to feel uncomfortable, I turned my head and had a good look at the man for the first time. He was an unkempt little fellow who looked very much out of place in this upper-middle-class apartment building. Everything about him looked gray — his suit, his eyes, his face, and his just-turning hair. He was a little gray man.

A horrible thought occurred to me. No, no, impossible. I couldn't have. I wouldn't have admitted a stranger into the lobby. I couldn't have been so idiotic as to hold open the door for a man who was following me. But my heart began to pound and I heard myself asking, "Do you live here?"

"Neow," he answered in a nasal twang. Even his voice was gray.

My heart pounded a little faster. "Are you visiting someone?" I asked. By now I had begun to believe that, yes, I could have been that idiotic, but I still entertained a faint hope I was wrong.

"Neow," he answered, and that was the end of my entertainment and my hope.

"What are you doing here?" I asked.

"I thought you and me could have a party."

Dumb Dora would have said, "Sure, you bring the pretzels." That would have made two Dumb Doras within the space of five minutes.

Trembling, I glanced around the lobby and observed four apartment doors. I readied my lungs for an emergency.

"I think you'd better go," I said as calmly as I could.

Said the little gray man, "I ain't never had no party before wid no dame what wears a uniform."

I got news for you, brudder. You ain't gonna have no party now needer wid no dame what wears a uniform.

What did he think would happen, anyway, with a

woman who wore a uniform — that maybe bugles would start blowing, first reveille, then taps?

Aloud I said, "If you don't leave, I'm going to scream."

"Come on. A party don't take long," he said, and with that he reached out to touch me.

I can only guess what his immediate objective was. I never really found out, for I swung out with my handbag and hit his arm. To my utter astonishment, he turned and ran out of the building.

By the time I reached the apartment, I was shaking like a street digger's electric drill. I went immediately to the phone and called the police. I started to tell the story to the officer who answered the phone, but he interrupted with, "I'll send an officer over right away, and you can tell him the story and give him a description of the man. What's your address and apartment number?"

I gave him the information he requested, and just as I was about to hang up, I remembered something.

"Oh, just a moment, officer. Your man won't be able to get into the building. I'll have to meet him in the lobby."

"All right. He'll be there in about five minutes."

During the next four minutes, I chain-smoked the few cigarettes I had left and then took the elevator down to the lobby just as the tall, handsome young man in the blue uniform came into the vestibule.

He introduced himself as Officer Williams, and he asked me to tell him exactly what had happened.

"I'm almost ashamed to tell you that I held the

door open for him myself, thinking he lived here. You see, I don't. I'm using a friend's apartment, so I would have no way of knowing who lives here and who doesn't. I began to get suspicious while we were waiting for the elevator and felt him staring at me. When I asked him if he lived here, he said no, he thought he and I could have a party."

"I see."

"I told him he'd better go, and he said he had never had no party wid no dame what wears a uniform."

"Is that the way he talked?"

"Yes. When I said I would scream if he didn't leave, he said, 'Come on, a party don't take long,' and he reached out to touch me, and I hit him with my bag, and he ran out."

When Officer Williams asked me what the man looked like, I described the gray little man as best I could, and he added the description to the notes he had already made.

"I hope you find him," I said. "I was lucky, but the next person might not be."

"I'll have a look around," said Officer Williams.

"Thank you for coming over, officer." I turned to go, then remembered I was out of cigarettes.

"Oh, officer, I wonder if you could do me a favor. I'm out of cigarettes. I noticed a tavern around the corner and I wouldn't want to go in there by myself, especially at this hour. Would you walk over there with me?"

"Certainly. Come along."

I bought my cigarettes, and on the way back to the

apartment, I realized I had stopped trembling. I felt so calm and so safe walking next to this tall, handsome man in blue, one of New York's finest. When we reached the street door, I said, "I'll be fine now. You won't need to come into the lobby with me. Thank you very much. I'm grateful," and I started to open the door.

"Just a moment," said Officer Williams.

I stopped and looked at him.

"Are you sure you wouldn't like to have a party?" he asked.

For a moment I stood stunned. Then I thought, "What an idiot I am. Surely the man is joking."

"Ha, ha, ha," I laughed.

But the officer didn't ha-ha back. For he was dead serious. He was looking at me waiting for an answer.

"Goodnight, and thank you again," I said and darted into the outer vestibule. Once more, I was shaking so I could hardly get the key into the lock of the inside door. I hurried into the lobby, and with a backward glance at the officer, who was still standing hopefully in the street watching me, I dashed into the elevator, which apparently had not been used since my descent. I got into the apartment and fastened the door — bolt and chain.

I ran to the phone and picked up the receiver to call the police, then promptly put it down. "What am I doing? That *was* the police."

Too overstimulated to go to sleep immediately, I sat on the brown sofa, covered my knees with the orange afghan, smoked cigarettes, and drank coffee.

After a while the trembling ceased, and I was calm enough to contemplate my two gentlemen of the evening: the gray and the blue. First I thought about the man in gray, and I hoped that despite the distraction, the man in blue would make an attempt to find him, for he could be a menace. Then I thought about the man in blue, and I laughed and laughed and laughed. I realized it had taken me all these years to discover what my third-grade reader meant by "your friendly neighborhood policeman."

Two days later, I was back in the safety of the war. I walked into the orderly room about five o'clock, and Lieutenant Brown, my Company Commander, greeted me with, "Am I glad to see you! I thought you weren't going to make it!"

"Make what? Is something wrong?"

"I have orders for you."

"Where am I going?"

"To OCS."

"No!"

"Yes!"

"When?"

"You're due there tomorrow morning. You'd better get packing right after mess."

I ran over to the barracks to deposit my bag and then over to the dayroom to call Peter. I dialled the BOQ number, and Peter answered.

"Hi, Peter."

"Rose? I've been calling you all day. When did you get in?"

"Just now."

"Did you have a nice furlough?"

"Just fine. I'll tell you all about it when I see you. And guess what, you won't have to push me into any more ditches. I'm going to OCS."

"That's great. Congratulations!"

"I'm a little scared."

"Don't be. You'll do just fine."

"I hope you're right."

"Of course I am. Oh, and-um, I have some news too."

"What's your news?"

"I'm going overseas."

"What! When?"

"I have to report in ten minutes. I'm finishing packing."

"That means I won't see you."

"I'm afraid not."

"I wish I had known. I could have come back a few days ago."

"I only found out yesterday, and I knew you were due back today."

"This is very frustrating."

"I agree."

There was a pause.

"Will you write and let me know where you are?"

"I can't promise to let you know where I am, but I will write. Take care of yourself."

"I will. You take care of yourself."

"I will. Goodbye."

"'Bye."

The next morning, at 0800 hours, a barracks bag

over each shoulder, a suitcase in my hand, and my heavy heart where my trachea should have been, I made my way to Building 66, Company One, First Training Regiment, for Officer Candidate Training.

CHAPTER EIGHTEEN

Shall We Dance?

For six weeks I was in Officer Candidate School. This made me an OC. Prior to entering OCS, we were Auxiliary Jones, Auxiliary Brown, Auxiliary Blumenthal. Now, we were OC Jones, OC Brown, and OC Blumenthal. We all had the same first name — Oasie.

All 150 of us were billeted in one building. We were twenty-five to a squadroom, six squadrooms, three up, three down. The classrooms were also in this building, where we learned more about mess management, supply, abbreviations, and all about the assumption of command.

Then there was map reading. I learned that an azimuth was something you draw, not drink. This gave me some concern, because drawing was not exactly my specialty. I remember my psychologist nephew asking me if I would take a test he was experimenting with that required me to draw the figure of a woman in profile. When he saw my woman, he chuckled (he was too polite to laugh). She was straight up and down. I had neglected to give her breasts. (Psychiatrists, don't write. I know, I know.)

But the concern I felt about map reading was nothing compared to the dither I was in about airplane identification. Beat me, starve me, take away my six-inch toothbrush, I couldn't identify airplanes. I knew every army regulation in the book and I could recite the Articles of War verbatim (well, almost), but I couldn't remember whether a B-24 had four engines or four tails. I was apprehensive about this handicap; if I couldn't distinguish an American B-24 from a German Dormier DO 17, it could be hazardous to my health. But even more important, I didn't want to be known as the class dummy.

My favorite subject was close-order drill, and here I knew I could show off my skills. (I had always been a good driller. Anthony, who couldn't do long division, became a great marcher.) When it was my turn to drill the platoon, in rapid succession I left-flanked and right-flanked and left-obliqued and right-obliqued and we went forward and backward and sideward — all the wards except up. I couldn't quite manage that one. I had a great time. Did my platoon have a good time? I don't know. They didn't say, although I did overhear one of the women whisper to her neighbor, "Screw her!" as she flung herself on her bed in total exhaustion.

Our courses were taught by the officers of the company, and they were good. They were good physicists, good department store executives, and good office managers, but teachers? — forget it! They didn't know their azimuths from their elbows.

Especially bad were their tests. Every good teacher knows the questions on a test should be clear, free of ambiguities, and not "tricky." The students may not know the answer, but they should at least understand the question.

One test we had was a beaut. I scratched my head, I bit the end of my pencil, and I used my eraser down to the metal. It was everything a test shouldn't be.

The officer who taught the course and prepared the test called the company together for a critique. She started with a harangue that would have shamed General Patton. We were stupid, we didn't study enough, we didn't belong in OCS, and on and on and on. We, the OCs, sat immobilized, too horrified at the injustice to move a muscle and too scared to speak up.

When she was through with her tirade, she announced that only one person had passed the test — Oasie Blumenthal, with a bare 70. I knew a moment of joy, but only a moment, for then I felt guilt at having betrayed my comrades by passing.

She then started the critique, and with each unclear, ambiguous, tricky question, my frustration mounted. I reached the point of saturation when my answer to a particular question was "Abraham Lincoln" and her answer was "Oranges." Emboldened by my moment in the sun, I decided I would be the sacrificial lamb, and I raised my hand.

"Yes, Oasie Blumenthal?"

I half rose and half froze and said, "I think . . ."

"In the army, you're not supposed to think! Sit!" she thundered.

Like lightning, I sat.

Shades of basic training! This was the second time I'd been told I wasn't supposed to think in the army. I sure hoped the enemies' armies weren't thinking either.

In the evening we did "girl" things. We washed our hair, we plucked our eyebrows, we manicured fingernails and pedicured toenails. We also wrote letters and sat around and talked. Mostly our conversation centered on what we would do if we "washed out." The most popular choices were "I'll die," "I'll kill myself," and "I'll go AWOL." The more we talked, the more nervous we became, until our fears were totally out of proportion to reality. So a few of us laid down the law. The word "washout" was verboten. Anyone who used this word would clean the latrines. So loathsome was this prospect that most of us wouldn't even risk uttering the word "wash." From that moment on, if someone had a leaky pen that stained her fingers, she would shampoo her hands, or launder her hands, or sanitize, lave, pasteurize — never wash.

The six weeks passed quickly, and it was now Friday, the day before graduation. Fifteen OCs had "washed out" (oops) — five from my squadroom. Five times had Lieutenant Landon appeared in our doorway and bellowed "Oasie So-and-so to the orderly room — ON THE DOUBLE." The sight of her would drain the blood from our bodies; then the name would be called, and the blood would return, but to one body less. Naturally we all commiserated with those who had failed, and I even felt sorry for Janet, the gal who had dated a gentleman friend of mine the night before we left Philadelphia — well, a little sorry.

This last day, however, we were jubilant. No one had been called during the preceding week, and we had been issued our officer uniforms, so 135 of us knew we had made it. We sang, we danced, and we breathed easily again. With my pal, Evelyn, I sauntered down to the PX and bought my gold bars to put into the pocket of my new officer-uniform in readiness for pinning on my shoulders the following morning.

At last it was Saturday, the day of graduation. Humming happily, I stripped my bed and danced over to the supply room to deposit my linens in accordance with instructions. In my cute little seersucker number, I scrubbed my last floor, and was getting ready for my shower when, suddenly, Lieutenant Landon appeared in the doorway.

"Oasie Blumenthal to the orderly room — ON THE DOUBLE."

I couldn't move. My legs were paralyzed, and my heart had stopped beating. The only part of me that was working was my brain, which was debating whether to weave carpets in Baku or repair bicycles in Shanghai.

I have no recollection of getting to the orderly room. I must have been propelled by some inner voice whispering a warning, "Yousureashellbettergetyourassinthereorelse." Suddenly I was standing in front of the Company Commander's desk. I became aware that two other OCs were standing next to me and that the Company Commander was saying, ". . . And you three are graduating at the top of the class. Oasie

Blumenthal, you will lead the company to graduation. Oasie Murphy, you will march in front of the second platoon. And Oasie Blackburn, you will march in front of the third platoon. Dismissed!

"BLUMENTHAL! DISMISSED!"

I scampered back to my squadroom, flung myself on my naked bed, and sang, "God bless America, land that I love." No matter that I sang in four different keys. (My competence in singing was on a par with my competence in identifying airplanes.) I didn't have to go to Baku.

An hour later, outside our building, I was at the head of the company. We were wearing our brand-new officer uniforms with the shining eagles on our brand-new kepis — at parade rest, ready to march to our graduation exercises.

With my eye on Lieutenant Landon for the signal to get started, I wondered whether, since I was not yet an officer, I dared use the authoritative, snappy commands reserved for them. Officers never said, "Attention" or "Forward march." They barked, "Atten-HUT" and "Forward HARCH" and "HUT-two three-four."

In the midst of my deliberations, I received the nod that meant, "Get the show on the road."

"Atten-HUT!" I bellowed, My command was so authoritative and so snappy that even Lieutenant Landon and a passing dog snapped to attention.

"Mark time, HARCH! Forward HARCH! HUT-two-three-four-HUT-two, three-four."

And so we harched. I harched in front, and the company harched behind me. Sometimes I harched backward to make sure the company was hutting on the right foot, which was really the left foot.

We harched and hutted until we came to a corner. Now, ordinarily, when I'm alone and want to make a right turn, I give my foot a little twist to the right, my body follows, and it's done. If I happen to come face to face with someone making a left turn, we do two steps to the right, two steps to the left, a little curtsy, a little bow, and the pas de deux is over. But this was no pas de deux. It was a pas de cent trente-cinq.

At the corner I had to wait for exactly the right moment. "Column right, HARCH!" I roared. The OC on the extreme right made a sharp turn and marked time in place while the OC next to her took one step forward while turning until she was abreast of the first, and the next OC took two steps forward while turning, and so on down the line until all ten were in a straight line and marching forward. The same thing was happening in the lines behind them, the entire company turning itself in a beautiful military parade formation. It was executed so well that in a different milieu, we might have been Rockettes. It's fun. Try it sometime with cent trente-cinq of your friends.

Twice more we had to do it — a column left, another column right, and we were approaching the place where the exercises were to be held.

The auditorium was on ground level of a red-brick building, and the doorway was just wide enough to admit the line of ten women abreast of each other. My instructions had been to march them into the auditorium, after which they could break ranks and take seats.

Now, this was going to be tricky. My "Column right" had to be given at exactly the right moment. A second too soon or a second too late, and someone would be marking time up against a red-brick wall, and then with the pile-up of women behind her — man, what a red, pushed-in face!

As we approached the building, my eyes were glued on that opening, and Lieutenant Landon's eyes were glued on me. She had just opened her mouth to give the command when I bellowed, "Column right, Harch!" and into the auditorium they swiveled.

It was magnificent!

I was brilliant!

There were endless speeches. They went on and on and on. At last, we stood up, raised our right hands, and swore we would support and defend the Constitution of the United States against all enemies, foreign and domestic, and we swore we would bear true faith and allegiance to our Constitution, and we swore that we took this obligation freely without any mental reservations or purpose of evasion, and we swore that we would well and faithfully discharge the duties of the office upon which we were about to enter. What the WAAC officer who was administering the oath didn't know was that I had been swearing for the past hour — "Get this damned thing over with."

At last it was over. With much excitement and laughter, we hugged, we kissed, and we pinned the bars on each other's shoulders. This done, Evelyn and I walked out into the Harch sunshine — Third Officers of the Women's Army Auxiliary Corps. When we saw two enlisted women (Auxiliaries) saluting, we both turned in alarm to salute the officers we had missed, and then we giggled like silly schoolgirls. We were the salutees.

Now there was only one more piece of unfinished business. We had to return to our squadrooms to await our orders. Several days earlier we had been given a list of five places available for assignment and had been asked to express our first, second, and third preferences.

I was pleased and even flattered that at long last someone was allowing me to think and recognizing I possessed the capacity for making a decision on my own. For so long I had been told what to do and where to go, so this was a gigantic step forward.

I had given the choices much thought. I eliminated Daytona Beach, Florida, as too hot, especially since we were approaching the summer, and I eliminated Camp Rustin, Louisiana, as too, too hot for the same reason. My first choice was Fort Devens, Massachusetts, as cool and close to home; my second choice was Fort Oglethorpe, Georgia — not so cool but also not so hot; my third choice was Fort Des Moines — what else was there?

My orders read, "Third Officer Rose Blumenthal atchd unasnd 1st WAAC TC Des Moine is reld fr dy Ft Des Moines Ia and will proceed on March 17 to *Daytona Beach* Fla reporting upon arrival to the Comdt 2nd WAACTC for asgmt and dy."

So much for making my own decisions. I guess I still wasn't too immersed in the ways of the army. I should have put Fort Devens last.

Because I wasn't due to depart for the land of my last choice until the following day, I had to spend another night in my old squadroom. Frustrated and angry, I rushed to the supply room to pick up bed linens to replace the ones I had just deposited; I made the bed I had just unmade; I unpacked the barracks bag I had just packed; and then I eyed the floor I had just arduously scrubbed. I thought of a couple of things I could have done to that floor which would have eased my frustration. But then I remembered I had just become an officer and a gentleman. So I just gave the bed a good, hard kick.

The following morning I unmade the bed, redeposited the linens, repacked my barracks bag, gave the bed another hard kick, and was on my way to the 2nd WAAC TC, Daytona Beach, Florida.

CHAPTER NINETEEN

Who's The Murderer?

Ten fledgling WAAC officers made the train trip to Daytona Beach. The most exciting event of this two-day ride was our stop at Jacksonville, Florida, where — what else? — we rushed off the train and took pictures of our wilting bodies in our winter uniforms.

We arrived at the Daytona Beach railroad station tired, dusty, and hot. Ten command cars, each with a third officer and an enlisted woman driver, were waiting for us, and as the names were called, each two-day fledgling was greeted by a six-week fledgling. We were birds of a feather.

Third Officer Norma Bailey was my bird. She was the Executive Officer of the Fifth Training Regiment, Fifth Company — my regiment, my company. Norma was twenty-five, blonde, and pretty. She had been in the Officer Candidate class before me.

"Hop in," she said. Hopping was not exactly what I had in mind in my olive drabs in this ninety-degree weather, but, having no choice, I hopped.

"How far is it to the fort?" I asked.

"It's not a fort," she answered. "It's a new encampment built for the WAACs, and it's called a cantonment."

"Oh. Sorry about that. How far is it to the cantonment?"

"Eleven miles. We'll be there in about fifteen minutes."

As we approached an area where all I could see was a large stretch of hot, white sand, I said to Norma jokingly, "I didn't know we had to cross the Sahara to get to the cantonment."

"This *is* the cantonment," she answered.

"What!" I shrieked. "But I wasn't issued any desert gear." I was no longer joking.

"I know. Tough!" she said good-naturedly.

As we proceeded farther into the desert, I could see small patches of grass hither and thither, and I felt a little better. I could also see, on one side of this desolation, a long row of wooden structures, obviously the buildings of the various companies: orderly rooms, supply rooms, mess halls and barracks.

Our car stopped in front of a low wooden building, obviously the orderly room of Company Five, Regiment Five. Anxious to meet my new Company Commander, and readying myself for the salute to my superior officer, I jumped out of the car and immediately froze in my tracks. Lying in front of the orderly room, on one of the thithers, was a snake — an ugly black snake as long as the Mississippi River.

My new Company Commander? The army must be getting desperate.

Since I have a lust for life, I was about to take to the

hills — on the triple, for (remember?) I was a good runner. I recall when playing softball once at a vacation resort, I was going from home plate to first base, and I heard a male spectator exclaim, "Wow! Look at Skinny run!"

During the next few paralyzing seconds, I asked myself several questions: Now that I was an officer, brave and true, was I going to be frightened by a low-lying snake in the grass? Was I going to be intimidated by a stupid reptile who ate bugs, lay in the midday sun, and didn't even know what an azimuth was? Hell, yes!

I was about to take off when Norma said, "Relax, he's dead."

I had no idea how she knew it was a he, but I was in no mood for inspecting.

"He can't be dead. He was about to attack," I said.

"Uh-uh. Your imagination. He's dead."

"I could see it in his eyes. I recognize that attacking look."

"His eyes are closed. He's dead, I tell you."

"Well, who killed him? What's he doing here? Is this some kind of joke? Is someone trying to tell us something?"

"I don't know. I don't know. I don't know. I don't know. We found him here this morning."

"Well, why don't you get rid of him?"

"We're trying. We've put in a request for someone to come and take him away. He'll be gone soon."

Su-r-r-re he will. The First Sergeant has to prepare a requisition that has to go to the Company Commander for endorsement and forwarding to the

Battalion Commander for endorsement and forwarding to the Regimental Commander for endorsement and forwarding, ad infinitum, and in the time it would take to get back from ad infinitum to the First Sergeant, I could make two pairs of lovely shoes and a matching handbag.

We skirted Pretty Boy Floyd, and I got to meet my Company Commander, First Lieutenant (Second Officer) Alberta Grant. She was thirty-something and good-looking, and as she extended her hand in greeting, I could feel her warmth. We chatted for a while, and then she briefed me on my duties.

I was to be the commander of the third platoon, with fifty recruits as my charges. In addition to daily drills, I was to inspect the barracks, inspect the women, and discipline them for infractions. I was also to be the supply officer for the company and teach one-third of the lessons. None of these duties posed any problems for me except the one she saved for last. Periodically, I was to be the officer of the day (OD— pronounced O-dee), a twenty-four-hour duty beginning at some pitch-black hour of the morning. The hour, of necessity, had to be pitch-black because the OD had to wake the CQ who had to wake the EW who were to be KPs.

Across the parade ground was BOQ (pronounced Bee-O-Queue), which meant Bachelor Officers' Quarters, where I was headed to get settled. "Um-m-m," I said to Norma, who was accompanying me, "interesting! Co-ed." She soon set me straight. Women's Officers' Quarters were also called BOQ.

Our BOQ consisted of a row of single-storied wooden structures, each containing about ten rooms. Norma showed me my quarters — no, quarter — it was still only one room. Nevertheless, I was in heaven. At last, after six months of big, wide-open squad-rooms, or cadre rooms which opened into big, wide-open squadrooms, I would be able to enjoy my longed-for privacy. The room was only six feet wide and nine feet long; the walls and ceilings had exposed beams; the closet was a doorless, curtainless, recessed area; there were open shelves on the walls for cosmet-ics, underwear, and various incidentals, including my mineral oil. But had this been a suite at the Waldorf, I couldn't have been more excited. I loved every inch of its drabness. True, I still didn't have my own latrine (it was down the hall), but I did have my own sink. I was on my way.

Now my recruits sat on their lockers, as I had done six months earlier, while I taught them the customs of the service, the wearing of the uniform, and the proper salute and read to them the prescribed Articles of War. I led them in military drill, inspected their barracks, listened to their problems, gave them help or solace, whichever the situation required, and disciplined them for infractions.

During this time, Daytona Beach was experienc-ing a heat wave, and I drank lots and lots of soda. If the soda machine in our dayroom was empty, I'd trot up to the company above or below, and if those machines were empty, I'd trot two up or two down.

One blistering day, there was a run on the soda

machines, and there were no sodas anywhere up and down the line. The pipes in BOQ were being repaired and the water was shut off, so not even water was available to me. (It figures. When else would they repair pipes but on the hottest day of the year?)

This thirst was threatening to drive me crazy when my eyes lit on my mineral oil. In desperation, I was ready to drink anything that flowed — so, trotting be damned, I reached for the mineral oil. Just as I put the bottle to my lips, water gushed from the spigot, and I cheated Montezuma of his revenge.

One day, as was inevitable, it was my turn to be OD. At five in the morning, I paused in the doorway of BOQ and gazed across the parade ground into the vast darkness. I had never realized before how black darkness is. I wondered what mysterious dangers lurked out there yonder in that murky nocturnal unknown.

I dragged myself away from BOQ and started across the bleak desert, my Boy Scout flashlight making small rings of light ahead of me as I gingerly put one foot in front of the other. I felt frightened and very alone, although on this particular occasion I preferred to keep it that way; never for one moment did the vision leave me of the dead snake that had greeted me on my arrival. Why, oh why, couldn't I have been assigned to battalion or regimental headquarters, where I could have sat in a snakeless room and just endorsed and forwarded?

Bravely, I plodded on. As I neared the barracks, I suddenly felt a sharp sting on my ankle. This was it! I was going to die! Now, I had been told many times that when one comes face to face with a snake, one doesn't run. But no one ever told me one couldn't scream. And scream I did, loud and clear — so loud and clear that the enlisted women, mistaking it for the "fall out" whistle, fell out of the barracks in their pajamas and into the inky-black morning.

Apparently my sense of pride, honor, and duty was stronger than my instinct for self-preservation, which, of course, was the sign of a good officer. I yelled, "No, no! Go back. It was only a snake."

The snake turned out to be a twig on which I had stepped and which had flipped up and hit me in the ankle. Yep! My strong sense of pride, honor, and duty was all for naught.

One day I received a letter from Bob, an old friend stationed at Camp Wheeler, Georgia, who had heard from mutual friends that I was at Daytona. He asked whether, because we were quite near each other (measured in army distances), I could get away for a weekend to visit him. I could stay at the guest quarters at the camp (latrines down the hall).

Bob was a Corporal, and I was quite aware of the rule of the armed services concerning social relations between officers and enlisted personnel. They were verboten. It wasn't a rule that was anywhere in writing. Neither the Articles of War nor Army Regulations mentioned it. It was actually a custom of the service that had sprung from the conviction that for proper discipline and effective operation, a person of authority must keep his distance. The custom had its origin in the premise that familiarity breeds contempt within an organization, but as handed down from army to army, it developed into a taboo encompassing the extracurricular relations of officers everywhere with enlisted personnel anywhere. So, since Bob was a Corporal and I was a Lieutenant, I would be in violation of a time-honored custom. But I rationalized that somewhere in those ancient customs there had to be one tucked away that made allowances for old friends and old relatives.

I arrived in Macon, Georgia, at noon on a Saturday. Bob, fresh from a parade at camp, met me at the railroad station. We had lunch, and then we took a walk through downtown Macon. I don't know where the Maconians were that day. Either they took to the safety of the hills on Saturday afternoons or they were lost in the waves of khaki that flooded the city. The soldiers were all over. They crowded the sidewalks; they filled the buses; they filled the restaurants and parks.

Macon on this Saturday was like Macon on any other wartime Saturday — with one difference. On this day, it had me. My presence there may not seem like a world-shaking event, and in any place but Macon, Georgia, it wouldn't have been. But Camp Wheeler had no WAACs. Most of the soldiers had never seen one, so the unexpected appearance of a WAAC officer on their very own streets was akin to an eighth wonder. Each soldier had to see me and each soldier had to salute me, and, as was the custom, I had to return each salute.

They came from across the street to salute; they

hung out of bus windows and saluted; they came out of restaurants; they came out of parks; and after saluting and passing, they ran back to approach and salute again. On and on they came, singly, in pairs, in platoons, from the mountains, from the prairies, from the oceans white with foam.

At first Bob was amused. Then he sympathized with my distress. He grabbed my hand and pulled me across the street and into a park. He found a bench partly hidden by a tree, and except for an occasional "Duck! Here comes one," we talked until dinnertime. The following day, I was quite happy to get back to the cantonment, unbearably hot as it was, to rest my aching arm.

I was stationed at Daytona Beach for three months. In early June, I received orders. I was going to Fort H.G. Wright, an army post, to be an executive officer with a WAAC detachment. This was exciting. True, it meant more women, women, women, but, hallelujah, also some men, men, men.

CHAPTER TWENTY

Sometimes North
Is South

At the Daytona Beach railroad station, I met the other two officers assigned to my company: Arlene, who would be Company Commander, and Sally Ann, who would be Assistant Company Commander. My designation as Executive Officer sounded important, but of the three I was the junior officer, low man on the totem pole.

Not unlike downtown Macon, Georgia, on a Saturday afternoon, the train taking us north was one big khaki crush. It made sardine cans look commodious. Although Arlene, Sally Ann, and I sat comfortably in two seats facing each other, GIs were sitting three and four in seats for two; they were in each other's laps; they crowded the aisles; they were curled up and fast asleep in the overhead luggage racks. We gals went to the lavatory in twos. One was for running interference.

In New York City, Arlene, Sally Ann and I detrained for the purpose of taking another train to New London, Connecticut.

"Why are we going to Connecticut when Fort Wright is in New York and we're already in New York?" asked Sally Ann.

Neither Arlene nor I knew the answer, but our orders read "To New London, Connecticut," so to New London, Connecticut, we went.

"I don't see any fort, not even a soldier," said Arlene, looking out the door of the railroad station in New London.

"I'll go over and talk to the ticket seller," I offered.

"Sir," I said, "we're three WAAC officers, and we're going to Fort Wright."

"OK."

"Do you know where it is?"

"Sure."

"Could you tell us why we're in Connecticut when Fort Wright is in the state of New York?"

"Because that's how you get to Fort Wright."

"But we came from the south, and we were already in New York. Everybody knows Connecticut is north of New York."

"That's right."

"So how come?"

"Fort Wright's on Fishers Island."

Terrific. First a desert with snakes all around, and now an island with sharks all around.

And Pauline thought she had perils!

"And what waters is this island in?" I asked.

Under stress I sometimes forget that a preposition should not be used to end a sentence with.

"Long Island Sound."

By this time, I'm ready to kill him.

"And where is Long Island Sound?"

"Look out the window."

Sure enough, there it was — a calm, peaceful body of water, and out there somewhere yonder was a place called Fishers Island, and out there on Fishers Island was an army installation called Fort Wright, and somewhere out there was the state of New York.

"Thank you, sir. Now all you have to tell us is how to get there."

"By ferry."

"And where do we get the ferry?"

"Just down the street a bit."

"Thank you. I'll get my friends," I said, and turned away.

"Lieutenant."

"Yes?"

"You can't get there any more today."

"Why not?"

"The last ferry left at four o'clock."

I looked at my watch. It was 4:05.

Now, for sure, I thought I would kill him.

"What do we do now?" I asked. "Swim?"

"Suit yourself."

"When's the next ferry?"

"Eight o'clock tomorrow morning."

"But we're due there today. Our orders specifically say so. We'll be AWOL."

"Lieutenant, I only sell tickets."

So Arlene called the fort, and we were instructed to stay at a hotel in New London and to come in on the eight o'clock ferry in the morning.

The last thing I heard from Sally Ann before she dropped off to sleep was, "I hope we get foreign duty pay for this."

The following morning we were on the ferry leaving the state of Connecticut, where we didn't belong anyway, and approaching the state of New York, where we did belong but where we weren't.

The forty-five-minute ride to Fishers Island was delightful. We stood on the outside deck enjoying the calm waters with nary a ripple and nary a shark in sight.

Part of the time we primped. The newspapers had been full of the receptions given to the first WAACs to arrive at an army post: hordes of soldiers throwing their hats in the air, rousing cheers, marching bands, enthusiastic photographers. Naturally, we were quite stimulated in anticipation of this overwhelming welcome, so as we approached the island, out came the combs, the compacts, and the lipsticks.

We stepped off the boat and onto shore with our faces ready with "say cheese" smiles. But the "say cheese" smiles turned to sour cream amazement, for there wasn't a soul in sight — no photographers, no soldiers, no bands, not even a kazoo.

"I'm sure he said the eight o'clock ferry," said Arlene.

But in a matter of minutes, we heard a rhythmic beat. Ah! that must be the marching band approaching. Around the bend a command car came bumpety-bumping, bumpety-bumping, and stopped at our

feet. It had a flat tire. Out jumped Private First Class
Ferguson, nervously trying to salute and apologize at
the same time and not having much success at either.
We finally decoded him enough to learn that he had
been sent to deliver us to our camp site and to tell us
that since the WAAC mess hall was not yet in operation,
we were to have our meals at Officers' Mess.

Well, that was a relief. At least we'd get a deserving
welcome from our peers.

After changing the tire, PFC Ferguson drove us to
the WAAC area. There were five buildings: the orderly
room and supply room with the WAAC officers' quarters above: three bedrooms, a bathroom, and a living
room adequately furnished and very nice indeed for
our *ménage-à-trois*. Behind this building was the mess
hall with its brand-new, shining ten-gallon pots. Opposite the orderly room, across an expanse of ground
large enough for company formations, were the usual
three barracks, each to house its *ménage-à-cinquante*
— *vingt cinq* up and *vingt cinq* down.

After we finished our inspection tour, it was time
for lunch, and we walked over to the Officers' Mess. As
we walked up the steps, Arlene said, "Brace your-
selves."

We stood in the doorway for a moment, looking
into the room where the officers of the post were
having their lunch. Bracing ourselves had been a total
waste of time. Not one officer lifted his nose out of his
soup, and not one officer stopped lying about how he
had scored while on leave. Zilch!

Three days later, our first contingent of thirty

WAACs arrived. *Now* Fort Wright burst into celebration; now were the GIs throwing their hats into the air; now was the cheering; now was the marching band. Only the fireworks were missing.

Every few days, more WAACs arrived, until we had our full complement of 150, and we became one big happy family — well, almost happy. Just as in basic training, there was always a Sylvia who didn't want to sleep next to Margaret, and an Elvira who didn't want to sleep next to Sybil. But mostly they were happy. They were proud to be WAACs proudly serving their country, and they accepted their assignments cheerfully: proudly the typists typed, proudly the clerks clerked, proud were the telephone operators, administrative assistants, cooks and bakers, and chauffeurs — chauffeurs who chauffeured the top brass and proudly saluted them, and chauffeurs who chauffeured the garbage and proudly held their noses.

And happily, they frolicked with the boys, and they organized bowling teams and baseball teams; and with them they put on a show called *It's All Yours, Buddy,* with singers, dancers, and a chorus line.

The show was written and produced by Corporal Sammy, a professional dancer of tap and other musical revue-type dancing. It was amazing how much talent we found among the GIs and the WAACs. Although in some cases the talent wasn't the greatest, it was compensated for by enthusiasm.

For six weeks, they hearsed and rehearsed, and I sat through every hearsal and rehearsal. I was advisor and supervisor, even though my total experience in these

SOMETIMES NORTH IS SOUTH   203

arts consisted of choreographing an Indian dance for an elementary school graduation.

The show was performed on two successive nights to Standing Room Only, and even the New London newspaper published a rave review. (It was written by a WAAC.)

It's All Yours, Buddy was such a success that I was asked to take it to the other four installations that composed the Harbor Defenses of Long Island Sound: three smaller islands plus Montauk.

We did Montauk first, which was a two-hour ferry ride from Fishers Island, and coming back the water was a little choppy. Several of my WAACs got sick, and I got sick watching them get sick, except I managed not to disgorge because I can't stand even my own disgorgement. (Notice I can't even write the v-word because if I wrote the v-word, I would surely v.)

After all the hearsals, rehearsals, and performances, I had seen the number called "The Misfits of the Battery" to the point of nausea. When we returned to the fort, I cornered Dorothy, a new WAAC officer stationed with us and the only officer thus far who was my junior. I gave her keys to the wardrobe room and said, "It's All Yours, Buddy." And there ended my theatrical career.

One day we received word that Colonel Oveta Culp Hobby, the WAAC Director, would visit us. For two weeks we scrubbed and polished. Even I scrubbed and polished as I hadn't scrubbed and polished since basic training and as I have never scrubbed and polished since.

Arlene and I went over to New London to escort her to the fort. It was exciting, sitting and chatting on the ferry with the Director of the Women's Army Auxiliary Corps. But it was even more exciting when, after she had inspected the WAAC barracks, inspected the WAAC mess hall, inspected our WAAC officers' quarters, and inspected our WAACs, she went into one of the WAAC latrines. I followed her in and went into the adjoining stall just so I could brag that I had shared a latrine with the Director of the Women's Army Auxiliary Corps. How many people can say that?

A couple of weeks later, we had another visitor: Lieutenant Colonel Grunert of the Eastern Defense Command. We had instructions in advance that Colonel Grunert wanted to see us in formation wearing our gas masks. The information we didn't get in advance was that he was going to call "Gas!" We had just received our gas masks the day before and had had time only for a short gas mask drill. So when the Colonel called "Gas," some women were adept, some were less adept, and some had ten thumbs. Before every one of us had finished donning our masks it had taken two minutes, enough time, we were told, to annihilate the clumsy. I would have been a dead duck.

On July 12, 1943, the Rogers bill was signed, which made the WAACs the WACs. We lost "A" for auxiliary and thereby gained free postage, six months' pay in death benefits, national life insurance, 20 percent extra pay for overseas duty, limited pay for disability incurred in the line of duty, and 50 percent extra for flying duty.

All WAACs who wished to be WACs had to re-enlist, and those who wanted out could leave. Of the 65,000 women then in the Corps, 14,950 chose not to re-enlist. There were three from our company, and when we received three replacements at a later date, one had been a WAAC officer who re-enlisted as a WAC private. Her reason, she told me, was that she liked the enlisted women better than the officers.

To become a WAC, it was necessary to undergo another physical examination. I could endure the physical part. What was I going to do about the color test? Where was I going to find another kind, sweet, sympathetic Major who would give me a "Boy, did we screw 'em" wink? How could I pass a color test if, in a department store, I seek help from any person within talking distance about the color of the sweater I'm considering buying? (Some help! The person usually answers with something like "Puce with a touch of canary," when all I want to know is — is it red?)

But I had to take a chance, sink or swim, and I made an appointment for the examination. The physical part went fine, and then came the color test.

This time, I was given a book that had on each page a group of colored dots, and hidden in these dots was a number.

"Tell me what number you see," said the doctor-Major, opening to the first page.

This was easy. There was the number four just as clear as though there were nothing else on the page.

"Four!" I called out jubilantly.

He looked startled, then turned the page.

"What number?" he asked.

"Seven," I answered without a moment's hesitation.

I found a number on every page. Something had happened to my color cones. I was no longer color blind!

Alas, my euphoria was short-lived.

The Major closed the book and in great excitement rushed into the next room shouting, "Ted, guess what! I just found a color-blind woman." It seems that the number four should have been a nine, and the number seven a three.

Lucky me. Again I was reminded that I was unique among women, for only one woman out of twenty is color-blind, compared to one out of twelve among the males.

But I was approved for the Women's Army Corps anyway, despite my color deficiency; in all other areas, I was in the pink — that is, I think it was pink.

I was sworn into the Women's Army Corps on Boston Common, in a small ceremony with 149 other officers. We were addressed by a Major General who warned us to regard our auxiliary service as merely the "honeymoon" of our army life.

Thanks, General. I'll pick my own kind of honeymoon.

The big celebration came when our enlisted women were sworn into the army. There was a band and there were troops and there were civilian observers from the upper end of the island and from New London. Once again I led the company. We harched and we right flanked and left flanked until we reached the portion of the parade ground where the ceremony was to take place. Major Dutton administered the oath. Our women raised their right hands as WAACs and dropped them as WACs.

During all this time, Sally Ann had been at Fort Terry, our installation on Plum Island, with twenty of our women. Sally Ann became ill and had to be hospitalized, and I was assigned to Fort Terry to replace her.

I liked this assignment. The women would drop into my office and confide their sorrows and their happinesses. Henrietta told me she was in love, and Emily told me she was in like. On Christmas Eve, I led the group into the Officers' Club to sing Christmas carols, and on other nights I joined the male officers at the bar, singing lustily along with them, "I've got sixpence, jolly, jolly sixpence" — in my four keys.

One day, I was notified there would be a formal inspection of the WAC barracks on the following Saturday morning by several of the male officers of Fort Terry.

Early Saturday morning, I went to the squadroom to make a preinspection inspection. Everything had to be perfect, and it was — almost. The twenty dark blankets with their six-inch cuffs were lined up to look like a row of penguins; all shoes and footlockers were faultlessly aligned; the windows glistened; the floor shone, for these women hadn't been satisfied only to scrub it, they had also waxed it.

Moving from bed to bed and nodding my

approval to each woman standing to the right of her footlocker waiting for the call to attention, I suddenly stopped. "Peggy, what's this spot on the floor in front of your footlocker?"

Peggy, horrified, exclaimed, "Oh, my God. It's a spot of wax. I'll get it this second." But at that moment, the WAC nearest the door called "Attention!" and the women, including Peggy, froze in attention position. I looked up to see three male officers: a Major, a Captain, and a First Lieutenant. I hurried to them and saluted, and the Major said, "Lead on, Lieutenant. We'll follow."

So I started — with three male officers in tandem behind me. Everything was going fine when suddenly something whizzed by me — a bat? — a bird? — a plane? Nope. It was the Major. His foot had found the spot of wax in front of Peggy's footlocker, and, propelled forward, he went loping down the room with his arms flailing wildly in an attempt to keep his balance. I could only stand there in stupefied horror as he loped on and on and on and into a WAC who fell backward onto her bed with the Major on top of her.

I was prepared for the worst: a furious harangue — a general court-martial — execution at dawn. But the Major was good-natured about it. "Too much wax," he said, removing himself from the WAC and rubbing his shins. I breathed again.

I was at Fort Terry about two months when the entire regiment was ordered to move out. Word was that they were going overseas. I remember standing in front of my orderly room watching the men march past as they left and waving goodbye to them. It was a sad time.

Fort Terry closed, and I took my WACs back to Fort Wright. By this time I had been stationed at the Harbor Defenses for about a year, and I was ready for a change, so I requested a transfer. At last I received my first choice — Fort Devens.

CHAPTER TWENTY-ONE

Yes! I Wore
Pink Underwear

I arrived at Fort Devens totally confused. I had received two sets of orders. The first set had named me Company Commander of the WAC detachment attached to Lovell General Hospital, and the second set of orders relieved me of my command as Company Commander of the WAC detachment attached to Lovell General Hospital and named me Assistant Company Commander.

After depositing my belongings in the quarters assigned to me, I reported to Colonel Martin, Commanding Officer and Director of Lovell General Hospital. He explained it to me. There were to be two detachments of 150 women each; they were to be situated about a mile apart and called North and South. Each section would have its own Company Commander, but the North officer would be *the* Commanding Officer. I was South.

Anxious to meet the Commanding Officer who had so unceremoniously dethroned me, I walked over to the North detachment and into the orderly room.

The First Sergeant told me the Lieutenant was expecting me, so I knocked on the door, walked in, and then stood there with my mouth wide open.

I couldn't believe it! Seated behind the desk was Terry Beasly, the pretty lass with the cherubic face and the flattering tongue who had been a raw recruit in basic training when I was a First Sergeant and who had plied me with Hershey bars and honeyed words to escape KP.

"Hi, Rose," she said. "I've been looking forward to your arrival."

Sure. Why not? To flaunt her silver bars and her superior position. I could see the smugness in her face.

"Hi, Terry," I answered. "How nice to see you," I lied.

How did she get to be First Lieutenant so quickly, I wondered. With Barracini chocolate-covered cherries, maybe? And what was that box of Godiva truffles doing on her desk? For sure, they were for the next rank up — Captain.

My company at South ran smoothly. My WACs were happy in their work, and we had good rapport. My problem was not with them — it was with Terry. It was bad enough that she was a First Lieutenant and my superior officer, she was also a bitch. I learned that she was in frequent communication with Major Alcott, WAC Director of the First Service Command, and, as overheard by one of her WACs and reported to me, she had told the Major that I was inefficient (not true), that I wore pink underwear (true), and who knows what else — maybe that I chewed tobacco.

I was glad I was a mile away; I was not anxious to tangle with this sycophantic biddy from Kansas City. I shuddered when I thought of how, as First Sergeant, my head had been turned by a smattering of flattering chattering, and how I had sold my soul for some handy candy with nuts. Knowing her as I did now, had she offered me any of her truffles, I would have insisted she eat one first.

Many of the WACs from North came down to South to tell me their troubles. When I told them I couldn't help them and that they would have to see Lieutenant Beasly, they complained that she was never available, that her door was always closed with instructions she was not to be disturbed.

Terry must have gotten wind of these visits, for one day she came to see me.

"Rose," she said, "I've decided that you will no longer be the Company Commander of South. Alice (the Supply Officer for both companies) will now be the Company Commander, and you will be the Supply Officer."

As if speaking to a third grader who had just been told she was going to be a tree in the Little Red Riding Hood play, she looked at me with those sweet, angelic eyes and said, "Don't think it doesn't take intelligence to be a Supply Officer, Rose."

So I looked at her with my sweet, angelic eyes and I said, "Up yours, Terry."

I scooted up to Colonel Martin's office and asked, "Can you transfer me out of the WAC detachment?"

"What happened?" he asked, and I told him.

"That figures," he said. "You're a threat to her. Actually, Major Alcott in Boston, the WAC Director, is the only one who is supposed to move WACs around. But I'll do it. I'll transfer you out and give you an assignment in the hospital. I'll also confide in you that I declared Lieutenant Beasly surplus, but Boston did nothing about it."

"Maybe they knew no one would want her," I offered.

"Maybe," he said.

"They could have tried the Army-Navy stores. They buy surplus, and they'll take anything."

We both laughed, and I felt better.

The Colonel picked up the phone and told Terry he was issuing orders transferring me out of the WAC detachment.

But now I had another problem: what to do about Major Alcott. She probably heard from Sleazy Beasly within minutes about my transfer, and she was not going to be happy about the disregard of her authority. So I went to Boston and told her the whole story. She was surprised. Terry had told her I had requested a transfer because I was miffed at not having been named the Commanding Officer.

The next week, I was a First Lieutenant.

CHAPTER TWENTY-TWO

Teardrops Keep Falling On My Handkerchief

Patients at Lovell General Hospital were for the most part returnees from overseas duty, some getting treatment for physical wounds and others for post-traumatic stress disorders.

Because many of these soldiers were ambulatory, they were permitted weekend passes and in some cases furloughs. My new assignment as Assistant Commanding Officer of the detachment of patients was to interview men who overstayed their leaves and recommend disposition, such as confinement to quarters, withdrawal of pass privileges, summary court-martial, or no punishment.

My first interview was with a young Corporal who was two days late from a three-day pass.

"Why did you come back late?" I asked.

His eyes became teary and his voice trembled. "I wanted to surprise my wife and when I got home, I found her in bed with another man. I just went crazy. I ran out and went on a binge for two days," he said as the tears ran down his cheeks.

"Excuse me a moment," I said, and I left the room, took out my handkerchief, and wiped my eyes.

Recommended Disposition: No Punishment.

My second interviewee was a twenty-three-year-old private.

"Why did you come back late?" I asked.

"My grandmother had a stroke. I had to take her to the hospital. I don't think she's going to make it," he added as the tears ran down his cheeks.

"Excuse me a moment," I said, and I left the room, took out my handkerchief, and wiped my eyes.

Recommended Disposition: No Punishment.

My third interviewee said his mother's house had burned down, and he had had to take her to Alaska to live with her brother. "She's not well. I don't know if I'll ever see her again," he said as the tears ran down his cheeks.

"Excuse me a moment," I said, and I left the room, took out my handkerchief, and wiped my eyes.

Recommended Disposition: No Punishment.

Interviewee No. 4 — No Punishment. His mother's house burned down too, but his mother's brother lived in Mexico.

Interviewee No. 5 — No Punishment.

Interviewee No. 6 — No Punishment.

In retrospect, I wonder how many of my interviewees thought, "I wish I had tried to sell her the state of Massachusetts."

At the end of one week, Colonel Martin called me to his office.

"Lovell is opening a convalescent center that will be located about a mile from here. I'd like you to run the office," he said.

I'm not sure whether he was enthusiastic about my capabilities as an administrator or disgusted with my softness with transgressors. But it didn't matter. I was running out of handkerchiefs anyway.

CHAPTER TWENTY-THREE

A Roll Is A Roll
Is A Roll

Convalescent Hospital was just the right place for me. I needed to convalesce. Here there were no unfaithful wives, no sick grandmothers, and no burned-down houses. Instead, we had a Colonel who was the Director and who did nothing, an Assistant Director who helped him, six psychiatrists, two physical therapists, a secretary, several enlisted men to act as aides to the doctors and therapists and to transport patients from Lovell to us, and there was I.

I set up schedules for the doctors and therapists, supervised the office staff (Edna), and when that great lady, Eleanor Roosevelt, came to visit Fort Devens, I even helped scrub and polish.

Among the aides assigned to us was a young Private First Class named Maurice. Maurice was twenty-three, handsome, and an imp. Every morning he would poke his head into the huge room that was my office and say, "Good morning, First Lieutenant Rose. How about a date tonight?"

"Go away, Maurice," I would order, and with a big

grin, he would disappear. Same ritual every morning.

Because my duties at Convalescent Hospital didn't really occupy me full time, every now and then I would get an additional assignment. Once I was Postal Officer for one day. Another time I was Library Officer for two days. Then one day I received a very unusual assignment: I was to escort a busload of GI personnel to a hockey game in Boston.

There were thirty-nine men with me on that bus. War sure is hell!

I was seated in the back seat between two enlisted men when along came Maurice and squeezed himself next to me. First thing I knew, he was holding my hand.

"Stop it, Maurice," I remonstrated as I pulled my hand away.

A minute later he had my hand again.

"Maurice, I said to stop it." Again I pulled my hand away.

After the fourth time, I walked to the front of the bus and asked a young man seated next to the window to change seats with me. I wanted a window seat so there would be no danger of Maurice walking down the aisle and grabbing my hand. In that way, I would be free of him.

It was still daylight, and I was enjoying the beautiful spring leaves that were speeding by when suddenly someone was holding my hand. I turned my head sharply, ready to rebuke my new seatmate, only to discover that I had a newer seatmate. It was Maurice. He had traded seats for a dollar!

All the way to Boston and back it was, "Stop it,

Maurice," "I don't want to hold hands with you, Maurice," "Stop it, Maurice." Nothing helped, so I finally gave up.

Was that the end of Maurice? Of course not.

During this time I was billeted with three other WAC officers in a stately red-brick house originally intended for married male officers. We kept only enough food for breakfast and ate our other meals in Officers' Mess.

One morning I was very late. I grabbed a few rolls and some coffee in a plastic cup and rushed to the office intending to have breakfast at my desk. As I entered the building, I ran into Maurice. Rushing past him, I asked, "Wanna roll, Maurice?"

"Sure," he answered, "Your place or mine?"

He had his roll. I threw one at him.

And was this the end of Maurice? Nope. The best was yet to come.

One morning I approached my desk and noticed, in its center, a folded piece of paper that was obviously a note. Still standing, I opened it and read, "If you got laid last night, smile."

There was no question in my mind who was at the bottom of this. I was outraged; this was going too far; it was insubordination; I would do something about it. And I did. I stood there and grinned. I had looked up and spied Maurice and a friend hiding behind a closet door with only their heads sticking out, grinning like two Cheshire cats, and I couldn't help it. *I* grinned like a Cheshire cat. Actually, I should have been crying.

One day I received orders to inventory the commissary. Me? Inventory the commissary? There must be some mistake.

It's not that I have anything against counting. I had had a lot of experience in counting. As a teacher, I counted noses every morning; I counted the number of minutes remaining to 3:15 P.M.; and I counted the meager dollars when cashing my salary check. But to count to 43,385 or thereabouts I considered above and beyond the call of duty.

I would go to Major Alberts and say, "I think, sir, you've made a mistake." Then I remembered my two unfortunate experiences with saying "I think" and their painful consequences. One doesn't say "I think" in the army if one cares for one's life. I realized, too, that the good Major would not appreciate being told he had made a mistake. Better to take a stab at the inventory.

The following morning, I said to Edna, our secretary, "I've arranged for you to be out of the office for a few days. We're going to inventory the commissary."

"Inventory the commissary, ma'am? Me, ma'am? I think . . ."

"In the army you're not supposed to think," I said, "Let's go."

Armed with an alphabetical list and Edna, I entered the commissary. There they were — wall-to-wall cans — big cans, small cans; round cans, square cans; tall cans, flat cans; blue cans, yellow cans, green, orange, and purple. I thought I would disgorge.

And so we started. There was allspice, anchovies,

angel food cake, apricots, artichokes, asparagus, and avocados.

Soon we got to beans. There were:

Great Northern — large, oval, pure white

Large, white — larger than pea, oval, pure white

Medium white — between small and large, oval, pure white

Small white — very small, oval, narrow, pure white

Pea — small, oval, round, pure white

Red Kidney — twice as large as medium white, kidney shape, red

Dark red kidney — twice as large as medium white, kidney shape, mahogany color

California red — medium, kidney shape, dark red

Pink — medium, flat, oval, light red

Pinto — slightly smaller than pink, kidney shape, buff specked with brown

After five days, that's what we were — dazed. As we walked to the commissary that morning, the only bright spot that illuminated our immediate future was the knowledge that we had already reached "rutabaga."

At last, with zucchini behind us, I shouted "Hooray!" and threw all the inventory sheets high in the air.

"Hooray!" shouted Edna as she jumped around catching the fruits of a week's horrendous labor.

Then we did a dance to celebrate our liberation. The dance? The can-can, of course.

We danced through the pouring rain, through the gigantic mudholes that had developed from the pouring rain, all the way back to our office. Exhausted and scarcely able to think straight, I flopped into Edna's chair and began to type — without paper. Edna flopped into my chair and began to type too, without a typewriter.

Along came Maurice. "Guess what?" he said.

"I give up."

"Convalescent Hospital is moving to Camp Edwards."

"This is not another one of your jokes?"

"No. It's official. We're going to be a bigger hospital. In addition to mental and physical therapy, we're going to have a training program, different kinds of activities for the patients."

"Where is Camp Edwards?"

"On Cape Cod, near Hyannis."

There was joy in Mudville that night.

CHAPTER TWENTY-FOUR

If You Value Your Leg, Don't Sit

We arrived at Camp Edwards in droves from the five corners of Fort Devens: the doctors with their tongue depressors and scalpels, the psychiatrists with their lumpy couches, the Red Cross workers with their cute little curtains for their windows in the barracks they would share with the WAC officers, the WAC officers with their envy of the cute little curtains the army wouldn't spring for, the Colonels with their smart secretaries, the physical therapists with their dumbbells, the enlisted men and women with their stripes and gripes, and the last and the most, the men who provided the reason for the existence of the Convalescent Hospital of Camp Edwards, Massachusetts — our overseas convalescing returnees.

What was my function in the above tableau besides being one of the WAC officers envious of the lace curtains? I was a teacher, and I had taught eighth-grade arithmetic. I became a supervisor of Commercial Education.

I had twenty-three instructors — enlisted men

and civilian women — who taught bookkeeping, typing, shorthand, real estate, sales, advertising, and business administration. My department was the largest. The others — woodworking, radio repair, auto repair, mechanical drawing, photography, and arts and crafts — were each taught by one person only.

Some of my instructors were pretty good, and some were pretty bad. None of them had any previous teaching experience.

So I took them in hand and gave them some principles of pedagogy. I told them about objectives, and the apperceptive basis, and the importance of reviewing at the end of a lesson; I told them always to ask the question first and then to call on the student and not the reverse; and then I told them my two pet peeves: don't just lecture, get your students involved, and don't sit unless you have a broken leg.

I must have been pretty effective. One day Susan, one of my instructors, told me that the night before she said to her husband, "What would you like for dinner? Would you give me the answer, please, Ronald?" And then she stood during the entire meal.

The student returnees were quite enthusiastic about the program. I often wonder whether some inspired young convalescent who sat in one of my classrooms eventually became another Billy Rose who won a national shorthand contest in 1917; and could Lee Iacocca have had his beginnings in my little white schoolhouse?"

When I heard we were to be inspected by the Commanding General of the First Service Command,

I wasn't surprised. We had had General Grunert and Colonel Hobby at Fort Wright and Eleanor Roosevelt with Colonel Hobby at Fort Devens, so why should Camp Edwards be any different?

General Sherman Miles was to visit us in a week. He was the most important military man in the northeastern United States. So there we were, scrubbing again.

The day before the General's scheduled visit, I gathered together my little crew of neo-pedagogues and I said, "Please keep in mind that the General is not coming to see you. He wants to see what our men are doing. In the typing classes, the men should be typing; in shorthand, they should be taking dictation; in bookkeeping, they're to keep books; and in marketing, business administration, and the other so-called lecture courses, be sure your students are participating. And one more thing: if anyone is sitting down while you're teaching, if your leg wasn't broken when you sat down, it will be when you get up."

One of my enlisted men instructors raised his hand.

"Yes, David?"

"You're lecturing, we're not participating, and you're sitting."

Wouldn't you know? There's one in every crowd.

The day of the General's visit arrived, and I stood at the door waiting in accordance with army protocol. Escorted by Colonel White, the Director of the training program, the General entered. I saluted, he saluted, Colonel White saluted, I saluted, and they started on their appointed rounds. I was asked to wait in my office.

While I chewed my nails, they inspected. Forty-five minutes later, they returned to where they had left me when I had ten fingernails.

I started to salute, but to my utter amazement, before I could get my hand to my temple, the General bowed, grabbed my hand, and kissed it. I was embarrassed, not by the kiss so much, but afterward I didn't know what to do with my hand. I didn't know of any army regulation that covered hand-kissing.

That evening, as I entered the Officers' Club, Colonel White grabbed me and hugged me. This was my lucky day.

"What gives?" I asked.

"Lieutenant, I salute you. Your classes were the only ones in which the students were working. In all the other classes, the woodworking, the repair shops, the mechanical drawing, in all of them, the instructors were lecturing, and the students were falling asleep. Come on, I'll buy you a drink."

Shortly thereafter, I became a Captain.

CHAPTER TWENTY-FIVE

We Never Forget Protocol

One of the ways the army personnel at Camp Edwards could entertain themselves was at the movies, especially since the movies were so cheap — fifteen cents.

One early evening I was standing on a long line with my friend and fellow officer, Ginger. The line was not moving; we were waiting for the first performance to end.

"Ginger," I said, "I have to go to the bathroom."

"Me too," replied my ungrammatical friend.

"Do you think they'll let us use the ladies' room before we buy tickets?"

"I doubt it," said Ginger.

"What'll we do? If we go back to our quarters, we'll miss the first part of the picture."

I pointed to a barracks building adjacent to the movie house. "What building is that?"

"That's a men's barracks building."

"Well, that lets us out."

"Maybe not," said Ginger.

"Hey, if you're thinking what I think you are, you're crazy."

"We could take a peek inside and see if anyone's there."

"Well, we have to do something," I said.

We left the line and hurried over to the barracks. We stuck our heads inside. There wasn't a soul around.

"Everyone's probably at the movies," I said.

"Do you think we can get back before the movie lets out?"

"It's going to be at least another ten minutes."

"Let's go."

The barracks were constructed not unlike the WAC barracks, so we found the latrine quite easily. We entered a large room which had a row of ten stalls on the right. Across from the stalls, on the left wall, was a row of ten urinals and nobody there. So far, so good.

Ginger and I each entered a stall, and soon I heard Ginger leave. I'm sort of like a camel, so I took a little longer.

I emerged from my stall fixing my skirt and preparing to look for a wash basin when, to my complete astonishment, I found myself facing a row of male backs, their fronts busily engaged! They had come in while I was flushing. I hadn't heard a sound.

One of the men, hearing me, turned his head and yelled, "Oh, my God!" and zip went his zipper. Up and down the line, heads turned and I heard, "Jeez!" and "What the hell?" and "Holy shit!" as zip, zip, zip, zip went the zippers.

"Don't mind me. I'm leaving," I said as I galloped

out as fast as my non-GI shoes with the high heels would allow.

I couldn't help feeling a little remorse when I heard one of the men yell, "Ouch!"

Ginger was waiting outside. "Why didn't you warn me?" I asked, not a little annoyed at my friend.

"How could I? When the men came out of the movies, they made for the barracks on the double. There was no way I could get to you to warn you. Did everything come out all right?"

"Everything went back all right, I think, except for one poor guy."

"What happened to him?"

"He got so nervous, I think he got caught in his zipper," I answered as we made our way to *Son of Lassie* with Peter Lawford and June Lockhart.

Camp Edwards became a comfortable place to be stationed. It was large enough to treat the dozens of returnees who arrived each day, yet small enough for the officers and cadre to have close rapport. We developed an intimacy that was almost homelike and enjoyed a pleasurable camaraderie.

Many of the married officers rented houses on the Cape outside camp so they could spend their off-hours with their wives, and as I got to know these officers, some of them invited me to their homes for weekends.

Captain Morris invited me to his home to spend the weekend with him and his wife, and I accepted.

Captain Goodman invited me to his home to spend the weekend with him and his wife, and I accepted.

Lieutenant Cornish invited me to his home to spend the weekend with him and his wife, and I accepted.

Major Stillwell invited me to his quarters to spend the weekend with him, and he had no wife. I said, "Uh-uh."

Despite my negative vote on his proposition, the Major and I remained good friends. Frequently we would spend an hour together at the Officers' Club just chatting. Mostly he would chat about how tough it was getting sex partners, and how miserable he was. Until one night.

We were standing at the bar, I with my whisky sour and he with his Campari, when suddenly he said, "Well, I finally scored last night."

"Oh, goody, I'll sleep much better tonight," I answered. "Anyone I know?"

"No. An enlisted woman."

"Oh? You fraternized."

"Yeah," he said, "Several times."

"Please. Spare me the details."

"But we talked too."

"That was nice. Did you ask her if she had read any good books lately?"

"How'd you know?"

"Oh, I've been around."

"She was a sweet kid. She asked me, 'Did you come, sir?'"

I tried hard not to laugh. "Well, you can't say we don't train our WACs well: remember protocol in all situations and under any conditions."

"And then she asked me, 'Will I see you again, sir?'"

"And?"

"I told her I didn't think so."

"That wasn't very kind."

"Oh, I thanked her for the orgasms."

"CLARENCE! ANOTHER WHISKEY SOUR, PLEASE!"

CHAPTER TWENTY-SIX

At Last
Good-Riddance

One day there was no more war. There was Hiroshima and there was Nagasaki, and there was no more war.

Along with the rest of the world, we cried, we laughed, we sang "God Bless America" and "I've Got Sixpence" and "I've Been Working on the Railroad," and we danced the Highland fling, the hora, and the can-can.

Eventually, the celebration had to be over. Serious business was at hand. We had to close down Convalescent Hospital, Camp Edwards, Massachusetts. Patients had to be transferred to other hospitals; civilian personnel had to be discharged; army personnel, enlisted and officers, had to be separated from the service or transferred to other units depending on each one's status.

Saying goodbye to my instructors was a wrench. We had grown fond of each other. I even liked David, who had reminded me that I should have been standing when I was sitting. Best of all, I remember Gloria.

She was one of my shorthand instructors, and she was black. She put her arms around me, and with tears streaming down her face she said, "Thank you. I shall never forget you. No one has ever been so good to me." So I put my arms around her and cried too. I cried for the parting, I cried for the emotion I felt at this touching tribute, and I cried for the implication of her words.

The Post Exchange had to close too. One of the GI employees hung out a big sign that read, "All Items Below Cost. Landlord Forcing Us to Vacate." Needless to say, there was a run on the PX that day.

I fought my way through the hordes and hastened to the perfume counter. There they were: for $.75, $1, and some as high as $1.25 — the Chanel Number 5s, the Crepe de Chines, the Shalimars, the Balenciagas, and innumerable others whose names escape me. So I did what any bargain-appreciative female would have done, I bought a few bottles. We-l-l, I bought thirty-two bottles. You name it, I bought it. (When I arrived home, my family and friends were the best-smelling people east of the Rockies. I gave my cousin Lil two bottles. On her way home to New York, she dropped them on the Forty-Second Street subway platform, and they smashed to smithereens. I still think she should have received a certificate of commendation from the mayor. The Lexington Avenue IRT subway smelled of lilac and hyacinth from the Bronx to the Battery for two weeks afterward.)

I was to be separated from the service at Fort Dix, New Jersey, but it would still be at least a week before

I got my orders. During the last week I was at Edwards, I went through my belongings in order to discard the items I would no longer need. It wasn't a very difficult task, because many of the items I had brought with me into the service I no longer had: such as, for instance, the alcohol, rubbing — it was gone at the end of the first week of basic training, when I had rubbed and rubbed my poor aching feet until not only the alcohol was gone but also damn near my feet; also, a few days on KP and my lotion, hand, was exhausted (and I was pooped). Nevertheless, there was still the mustard-colored underwear, the almost-brand-new GI shoes, and, of course, the mineral oil. The underwear and the shoes were no problem. I sent them to a charitable organization. But what about the mineral oil? For almost four years I had lugged that damned bottle around with me. From time to time, I had tried trading it for cigarettes — a carton — a half carton — one pack — one cigarette. Never had a taker. Sometimes, on a change of station, I'd deliberately leave it behind in the hope that someone who could use it would find it. Someone always did find it and came running after me yelling, "Hey, you forgot something." I considered pouring it down the drain, but my conscience warned me it would be a waste and a sin, considering that all over the world there were thousands of people suffering from irregularity. So I did the only thing left — I drank it. It worked out fine, though, because that last week I was merely sitting around waiting for my orders to Fort Dix, and it didn't matter where I sat.

On one of those last days, I ventured into Boston for browsing and shopping. I was standing on a curb waiting for a light to change from red to green, my Good Conduct and American Theater of Operation ribbons over the left pocket of my Eisenhower jacket and my Captain's bars gleaming in the August sunshine. Suddenly I felt someone touch my hand, and I looked down into the face of a little wrinkled old lady. She must have been at least ninety. She wrapped her bony hands around my left hand, looked up at me with glistening eyes, and said, with tremendous passion, "Thank you, oh, thank you, for winning the war. God bless you."

I can't begin to describe my feelings. I only know that by the time I reached the other side of the street, I had tears in my eyes. I felt unworthy of such deep gratitude, even though I was aware it wasn't a personal tribute, but rather, through me, a tribute to all the fine men and women in all the services who had given so much and who had helped achieve victory for our country.

During my service, I experienced inconveniences and privations. But I have long since forgotten them, for there were many rewards. With the wearing of the uniform of the Women's Army Corps came a sense of gratification for making a contribution to the war effort; by virtue of having worn the uniform, there were educational benefits of which I was able to avail myself; wearing the uniform meant never having to say, "I'm next," because whether in a crowded bakery or on a movie line, the uniform was always served first.

Yet I know that of all the rewards I received for the three years, nine months, and eighteen days I spent in the service, my greatest reward came from a little old lady on a street corner in Boston who said, "God bless you."

*   *   *

And now, what about Peter? Well . . . we corresponded all the time he was overseas. When the war was over, Peter came home and we were married — he to Marian, and I to Sidney.